Talks My Mother Never Had With Me

Helping the young female transition to womanhood

Dr. Ollie Watts Davis

KJAC Publishing
P.O. Box 111
Champaign, Illinois 61824
www.kjac-publishing.com

About the cover
The tear-away (heads missing) is the motif of the **Talks Mentoring** curriculum series, and symbolizes the wisdom that is not being shared between mature adults and today's youth. This photograph includes Martha Bunch with her daughter, Elisabeth; and Ollie Watts Davis with her daughters: Ashley (seated left), Charity (seated front) and Kirstie (standing on the right).
Art direction and design is by CarltonBruettDesign.

For mentoring training videos and additional materials for young people, contact KJAC Publishing by writing the above address or call toll free **1-800-268-5861**. You may also order f rom our web page: **www.kjac-publishing.com**

Acknowledgments

I am delighted to acknowledge the help I received in bringing this book through to completion. Many people were invaluable to this project—the pray-ers, the encourage-ers, the read-ers, the re-read-ers, the listen-ers and the hear-ers. Thanks to all who prayed, offered encouraging words, wrote letters, sent cards, e-mails and faxes. I thank God for you.

To my family, especially my four children (Kirstie, thanks for the beautiful *Introduction*, Jonathan, Ashley and Charity), who released me to pour much energy into this writing project, who provided inspiration for much of the content material and who always made mention of this book in your prayers, thank you. I was incredibly strengthened by your intercession. I am not sure that I should thank my husband, Rev. Harold Davis, or not. Writing a book under his commission is more than a notion! (I love you, dear!)

But God is faithful and provided exactly what I needed just at the right time to accomplish what He commanded—Casey Jo Ahn Robards, my principal editor. It is often said that opposites attract. In our case, we are wired about as differently as two humans can be—in temperament and talent. She is low key, I'm high strung, but we both embraced the importance of this project, committed ourselves to communicating directly and forged an unlikely partnership. It was this pure motive and purpose that made our working together quite extraordinary. Thanks Case, your timing is incredible—right words at the right time, clear vision in cloudy circumstances and gentle strength at all times. Truly, the fellowship of kindred minds is like to that above. Thanks for teaching me how to receive. I love you.

Soli Deo Gloria!
(to God alone be all glory)

Ollie Watts Davis

Contents

Introduction

U pon being asked to write this introduction, I was elated. This was more than an opportunity. It was an honor. The privilege and fortune to fully preface this compelling compilation of indelible ideas is quite an awesome responsibility. Knowing that what I write can influence your opinion of this book, makes me think carefully about the purpose of this introduction.

Oftentimes, I think about those young ladies who grew up without a mother who talked to them. What if I was one of those young ladies? (What if you are one of those ladies?) What if an older woman were to share her thoughts on the purpose of living—how much wisdom you would gain just by listening? Who would not be blessed by such conversation?

Listen to me. The talks in this book will benefit you for years to come! You may ask, who am I to tell you this? Listen to the author's oldest daughter, to my side of the story.

It gives me great pleasure to introduce you to my mother, Dr. Ollie Watts Davis. Come with me into the wonderful world of womanly wisdom given to Dr. Davis by her mother and mentors, and gained from her methods. This wisdom is tried and true. It will give you understanding beyond your years. I truly treasure the fact that you understand the importance of wisdom because you show interest in this book.

Do you know someone who has influenced you in such a way that you want to imitate them? Think about it. Of course you do. Maybe you see these special men and women on a consistent basis; they're part of your circle of contact. Others, you admire from a distance. My mother is that special someone in my life. She is the one I admire from up close and at a distance.

My mother has a standard of character that is exuberantly expressed in all she does. Her life is a wonderful witness. I know her as a wife to one, a mother of four, a mentor to many and a musician to most. I could talk about her faithfulness to my father, or her perfection in the performing arts, and go on forever about how wonderful she is in those areas. Although her marriage and career carry as much weight as her motherhood and mentoring, I will share my thoughts on what she does as a mother and mentor.

As a daughter, I have been bountifully blessed. Not just with a mother in the household, but with a friend, role model and mentor, need I say more? She is truly a treasure in my life. I've known her for eighteen years, and have not seen her do anything that did not benefit our family. In her ways and in her words, she is Grade A mother material.

I see my mother work with students on a regular basis. I see her as a mentor to both young and old college women on campus. They come see her all the time, for an encouraging smile that brightens up whatever situation they're in, to hear a helpful hint that reminds them of their purpose for going to school, or just to have someone who will listen to their problems. I honestly do not know how many women she has helped. With only an encouraging word or look, she can meet them where they need help the most. I sincerely love that about her. She helps these young ladies freely, which is such a fine attribute.

Many times I think about what she tells these young ladies. I think about the fact that I am expected to know all of these things. I think about what would happen if I slipped slightly—what would be said of her, or of me. I know that a tree is known by its fruit. I think about a lot of things, I know. Why would I go against motherly wisdom? Why would I try to do anything that did not align with what I've been taught? To me, that is ridiculous. That's just asking for the wrath. Many young ladies have grown up as blessed as I am, but think something different and unfamiliar is better. Deep down inside they know what their mother told them was right.

Have you ever heard the phrase, *common sense is not so common?* Unfortunately, this is true in contemporary society. What was common thirty years ago, in that the young learned from their elders is not so common today. Our society has reached a point in which the old and wise do not talk to the young and inexperienced. The generations have grown apart, which makes it difficult for the young to gain understanding from the old. Many girls do now know what they are missing—that they need an older woman, a mother or mentor, to guide them in the right direction. This book provides an opportunity for older women and young ladies to regain the bond they once had in years past.

Talks My Mother Never Had With Me is comprised of personal stories and is a great source of knowledge for elders to share with our young. It is a rare realm of rhetoric with a simple purpose: to reveal what an older woman wants to share with the next generation.

I can continue to tell you how much this book will enrich your understanding, but it's your turn to read this richness for yourself. Then you will not only hear about this wisdom but you can begin living a life of wisdom. You have this book as a resource. Read this book, write in it, learn the principles and share them with others. What more can I say?

Kirstie Elisabeth Davis
(her first-born)

My great-grandmama told my grandmama the part she lived through that my grandmama didn't live through and my grandmama told my mama what they both lived through and we were supposed to pass it down like that from generation to generation so we'd never forget.

Gayl Jones

Foreword

I seldom conclude a conversation without at least one reference to my mother. I will either quote her directly or in paraphrase. Her words are so much a part of me that I am hard pressed to differentiate between what I conceive and what is my mother. I am very indebted to this great lady.

Although they've never met her, my husband, children, friends and students are intimately acquainted with my mother through me. Ramona Sereta Crider Ross was a legend. She was larger than her own life. Her words are as appropriate for those I love as they were for my siblings and me.

I have used the counsel that I received from my mother to counsel countless others. For many years my husband, Rev. Dr. Harold Davis, encouraged me to multiply my efforts by making my talks available in print. I can't count the number of times I shared points with him and heard him enthusiastically say, *"that would make a great chapter in your book."* I would just smile and nod in agreement, but my words never made their way to paper. There was really only one thing that kept me from writing. One condition had to be met before I committed to writing a book—I didn't yet feel the need to write a book.

My writing could only be in response to my need to express myself. The need finally came. In addition, three points had to be agreed upon. First, I had to benefit from what was written. I wanted to be able to come back to the book time and time again and be encouraged by its contents.

Second, the book must reflect my personal experience. I didn't want to write an autobiography, but it had to be real. I was not interested in writing theoretically or making commentary. I wanted to add personality to the principles presented. Third, the tone must be positive, optimistic and conversational. I wanted the reader to feel like she had a private audience with the writer; as if we were talking face-to-face, person-to-person. Rev. Davis agreed to the condition and points, and work on *Talks My Mother Never Had With Me* began.

This book is about a mother and her talks with her daughters and sons. The talks that a mother has with her children protect them, provide for them and prepare them for what is upon them and before them. My mother talked to me. I pray that I have written here my gratitude to her.

Part I

Dealing With Your Past

Know whence you came. If you know whence you came, there is really no limit to where you can go.
James Baldwin

1
Understanding Your Orientation
(how you came to be)

You are probably not old enough to recognize how much you act, think, talk, walk and look like your mother. When I was your age, I couldn't see any resemblance either. Others saw it, but I didn't. I can't count the number of times I grew up hearing, "Girl, you just like your Mama." But just keep on living. I literally scare myself now with how much I am like my mother. I'll be talking to one of my children and not only will her words come out of my mouth, but her tone of voice as well. And don't let me pass a three-way mirror in the mall and catch my side-view, child, it's frightening!

My children never had the opportunity to meet their maternal grandmother, but my siblings tell them that I am just like her. And I admit it, I am. (I am a lot like my mother.) For 17 years, I watched her. I listened to her. I learned from her. She provided me with my education for life and living. I had the benefit of wisdom that came from our age difference. Many times I heard her say, "I've been where you're trying to go," which always meant that her advice had been tried and could be trusted.

My mother provided me with my introduction to the world—my orientation. Orientation includes your life commandments, norms and ways of thinking and behaving. The way she raised me and my brothers and sisters gave me a framework from which to operate. This framework really came into focus when I had my own children.

An example from my own orientation is my work ethic. I attribute my work ethic to my mother. While she did not work outside of the home, she taught me that the world didn't owe me anything. I had to work for what I wanted. I learned early that you had to pay your own way. Another example from my orientation that is clearly evident in my attitude and behavior with my own children is my emphasis on education. My mother taught me the value of a good education. "Get something in your head," she would say. "If you get it in your head, no one can take it from you. Get as much as you can, go as far as you can go."

My brothers may have had a paper route, cut a neighbor's grass or picked and sold blackberries, but none of us had steady jobs during the school year. My mother and grandmother fed, clothed and provided shelter for us. We were not expected to provide for our necessities. Our job was to focus on doing our very best in school. We were encouraged to be active and enjoy school. I remember my mother once saying, "Don't rush into getting a job. Once you start working, you'll work for the rest of your life. Your schoolwork is your job."

She didn't only talk the talk, but she walked the walk. She was involved with my education. She attended the parent-teacher conferences. She was a member of the PTA. She was there for the spaghetti dinners, wrapping the May Pole, and when she thought justice had not been served to one of us. On more than one occasion she showed up at school to talk to a teacher. I am the beneficiary of her involvement.

The things my mother taught me are innumerable. I could go on and on, but I think you get the point. I have shared these things to get you thinking about your own orientation. To what extent have your parents, your mother in particular, shaped you? How has your personality been stamped? What have you learned from your orientation? You may not see the influence of your orientation. But you are wearing it like an old dress or suit of clothes. Others see it right away through your attitudes and actions.

There is no greater study to undertake than the study of your orientation—how you were raised. Everyone should think about why they are the way they are—what those who raised them did right or wrong. Such knowledge is practical and useful. It is not only good for you, but those who come in contact with you will benefit from your understanding.

Many wait until they have had some traumatic experience as an adult before they seek to understand how their upbringing has shaped them. If you have had problems in school, are accused of being negative and disagreeable, or if your means of communication includes yelling and screaming, find out why. I strongly encourage you to start your study right away.

Now that I've got you thinking about your orientation, let's go further. Merely thinking about how you were raised is a good first step, but it doesn't accomplish understanding. To understand yourself, you must know about all of the pieces of your past. To just deal with your present attitudes is to only address the surface of your personality. You have to get down to what motivates your behavior and beliefs—the WHY of your personality. To get started, take this self-test:

1. *Reconstruct your orientation family.* Who were the primary members? Your family is the most powerful resource for your survival and success that you will ever have. In the

African-American context, family means more than just your nuclear family (mother, father, brothers and sisters). Family to black folk refers to whoever is in the "household," and includes those extended out into the community as well. Sociologists call these members *fictive* relatives—people not related by blood, but accepted as family and for all intents and purposes treated as family. I remember having some "aunts" that weren't kin but who were considered family. Who were your *fictive* aunts?

2. *What was your relationship with each member of your family, particularly the female members? What sort of influence did each member have on you?* Can you trace any of your actions and attitudes back to someone you remember from your childhood? There is a strong tendency within all of us to mimic the behaviors and attitudes that we grow up with, whether they are destructive or constructive. Two African philosophical tenets support this.

> *The individual does not exist alone but rather cooperatively and collectively. Thus whatever happens to the individual happens to the whole group, and whatever happens to the group has an impact on the individual.*

> *I am because we are, therefore, I am.*

3. *What woman served as your role model? Whom did you want to be like when you grew up? How did they deal with disappointment? How did they deal with anger?* You have been around a lot of women in your lifetime. From some of them you have learned what to do and from others you have learned what not to do. Are you aware of this? Promise yourself that you will do all that you can to deal with negative attitudes and destructive behavior as soon as you are aware of it, regardless of where you picked it up from.

My mother was my principal role model while I was growing up. At different points in my life I have learned from other women, for whom I have great respect. But it was my mother who really made the greatest impression on my personality and impact on my life. She wasn't perfect. Nobody is. But with all of her imperfection, I rise up and call her blessed.

I honor my mother because she was real. She knew that she had blown it in some areas and she cared enough about me to be transparent and honest. I appreciate her accepting responsibility for her actions and not trying to justify poor choices. When it comes to mothering, she is my role model. My children benefit from her commitment to raising me and my brothers and sisters. She was a skilled, loving mother. I hope that I do as well with my children as she did with hers.

You may not be able to see any good that's working on your behalf right now. I haven't always had the perspective I have now concerning my orientation. I have had a range of emotions— embarrassment, shame, anger and denial. To deal honestly with your orientation is part of growing up. It is something that we all have to do. And growing up can hurt your feelings. It is painful to realize that everything you came up with hasn't been good for you. But that realization starts a healing process. I want to share with you some steps I took that helped me heal.

Step 1. Choose a wise, older sister to confide in. Everybody needs somebody that they can talk to. (somebody who will listen and not judge them or try to solve the problem) You need an older, wiser woman who has life experience and some strict, well-thought-out, wise principles for living. Don't talk to just anybody. Seek out someone you respect, who has her act somewhat together. You want to hear some wisdom about life, not just a lot of words. Look for wise counsel.

Step 2. Choose the right friends. Your friends need to have a desire to do what is right. You can't get your act together and hang out with people who don't have their act together and aren't concerned about it. Associate with girls who will put positive pressure on you. Look for good, healthy companions.

Step 3. Keep your mind and thoughts clear. Don't try and avoid reality through any means of escape. Keep your senses sharp and stay alert. Beware of the legal and illegal forms of substance abuse (alcohol, drugs, cigarettes, etc.). Remember, not everything that is lawful is good for you. It may be legal, but it is not moral. Smoking cigarettes or drinking beer, wine coolers and liquor won't send you to prison, but it can imprison you in another way. You will become a prisoner of your own body's cravings.

Don't fall for the lure of the media (the glamor and glitz), instead go to the funeral of a teenager killed by a drunken driver or attend a M.A.D.D. (Mothers Against Drunk Drivers) Rally and see reality.

Step 4. Identify your areas of strength. Focus on your gifts and talents. Whatever you do, do it to the best of your ability, with all of your might and strength. Develop yourself to your full potential. Everyone takes pride in accomplishment. Your skills and abilities will guard you against feelings of low self-esteem. To be successful at anything requires determination and commitment to doing whatever it takes. In other words, you must be willing to work hard at what you want to be and do. Share your talents by helping someone else. There is no greater sense of self-worth and esteem than from knowing that someone's life has been enriched by your efforts.

Questions

1. Has anyone ever told you that you look like your mother?

2. The author states that you wear your orientation like____.

3. To what extent do you feel that you understand your orientation?

4. Are you afraid to talk about your past?

5. What emotions come to mind as you think about your past?

6. How do you feel your family has prepared you to survive?

7. Have you looked at the *why* of your personality?

8. What good or bad habits have you picked up from your family and fictive family members?

9. Do you plan to wait until you arc an adult before you begin to assess how you were raised?

10. Can you see any good in your orientation right now?

11. What are your strengths?

12. What are you doing to develop your strengths?

13. Who is helping you?

Mother Wit

Listen carefully to what the country people call mother wit. In those homely sayings are couched the collective wisdom of generations. MAYA ANGELOU

If a child lives with criticism, she learns to condemn.
If a child lives with hostility, she learns to fight.
If a child lives with ridicule, she learns to be shy.
If a child lives with shame, she learns to feel guilty.
If a child lives with tolerance, she learns to be patient.
If a child lives with encouragement, she learns confidence.
If a child lives with praise, she learns to appreciate.
If a child lives with fairness, she learns justice.
If a child lives with security, she learns to have faith.
If a child lives with approval, she learns to like himself.
If a child lives with acceptance and friendship, she learns to find love in the world. DOROTHY L. NOLTE

To do good things in the world, first you must know who you are and what gives meaning in your life.
PAULA P. BROWNLEE

You need to claim the events of your life to make yourself yours. FLORIDA SCOTT MAXWELL

The kind of ancestors we have is not as important as the kind of descendants our ancestors have. PHYLLIS A. WALLACE

It's a great satisfaction knowing that for a brief point in time you made a difference. IRENE NATIVIDAD

2
Nurture and Admonition
(the way you should go)

You can probably live without one more person saying anything to you about your attitude. As far as you are concerned, there is nothing wrong with your attitude. I feel you. When I was an adolescent I wasn't hearing it either. But fortunately, there were people in my life who kept talking to me. They would not leave me alone. They knew what I didn't know—that a good attitude would take me far in life, that I couldn't afford to have a bad attitude and that I needed to know how to get along in order to get ahead. At the time, it really got on my nerves, but I appreciate them for it now. Do you have people in your life that will challenge your attitude?

This talk about your attitude may get on your nerves, but I can't leave you to yourself on this one. You may not need to change anything but you do need to take a look at how you are coming across to others. Do me a favor and just hear me out. Better yet, do yourself a favor and answer the following questions.

1. Does the mention of the "A" word (attitude) make you want to roll your head, roll your eyes, have someone 'talk to

the hand' or snap three times in the air?

2. Is it necessary for you to be loud in order to be heard?

3. Do you need to be the center of attention?

4. Do you feel that attention from negative behavior is better than no attention at all?

5. Are you afraid to open up to anyone because you fear rejection?

6. Are you uncomfortable with receiving compliments or platonic hugs (friendly embraces, with no romantic intentions)?

If you answered yes to any of the above questions, this chapter is for you.

Attitude is that part of your personality that is revealed through your behavior. It starts at the feeling level with your emotions and then works its way out in what you do and the way you do the things you do. Your attitude needs to be nourished in a positive environment. It is not enough to just be fed physically. You must be sustained emotionally, spiritually and intellectually in an atmosphere rich in encouragement, tenderness, patience, listening, affection and love. This is called nurture. Nurture is to the personality what nutrition is to the body.

The ties that help to develop our personality are the close, personal type, most importantly, the mother-daughter bond. Being hugged, held, cuddled, kissed, talked to, and sung to start us out right and keep us healthy emotionally. Love and human contact are as basic a need as food to our development. It is believed that we all need at least 7 hugs a day in order to feel healthy. Have you been hugged lately?

As you get older, the ways in which you are nurtured may change. You may be cheered on at a ballgame, supported at a play, musical, or other important function. You need praise for what you do well and encouragement in your weak areas for your personality to grow. Support builds all your self-stuff—self-confidence, self-concept, self-esteem and self-worth. When was the last time you were told that you did a good job?

There were many that encouraged me when I was coming up. My mother, grandmother and godmother were the principal builders of my character and confidence. I carry my grandmother's first name, my godmother's middle name and my mother's image—if you've seen me, you've seen my mother. These three strong women were committed to seeing me become all that I was created to be. I give thanks daily for the time and effort they spent pouring attention and affection upon me. I am secure as an adult because they made me feel so significant as a child. They, as well as my sisters and brothers, provided me with the nurture I needed at home. My oldest sister Linda still calls me her baby to this day!

I had the benefit of coming up with women who knew that teaching was their calling. Outside of my home, others who saw potential in me and stayed on me until it was worked out were Mrs. Ethel Caffie-Austin, my mentor; Mrs. Gloria G. Carper, my adopted *Mom* (who encouraged me tremendously as a newlywed and continues to encourage me to this day); Mrs. Eunice Fleming, (who taught me geography, music appreciation, chorus, was my basketball coach throughout high school, and still supports all of my activities); and Mrs. Gladys Wheeler, my 1st/2nd and 3rd grade teacher. Mrs. Wheeler had to use all of her resources and then some to deal with me when I entered her classroom. Let me tell you what I mean.

When I entered first grade, I was a social butterfly—an incessant walker and talker. I still have my progress report cards that tell my story.

1st Six Weeks: A/B Honor roll. Ollie is making good progress, but Ollie walks too much.
2nd Six Weeks: A/B Honor roll. Ollie continues to do good work, but Ollie talks too much.
3rd Six Weeks: A/B Honor Roll. Ollie is doing above grade level work, but Ollie continues to walk and talk.

And so this continued day after day—good academic work with lots of socializing. I wasn't a troublesome child, I just wanted to visit with everyone, and not only at recess time. But, Mrs. Wheeler, being the master-teacher that she was, knew how to deal with me with wisdom and knowledge, and according to my personality. My classroom was a lot different from yours. There was one teacher. No aides. Three different grade levels (1st, 2nd, and 3rd), and who knows how many ability levels. The teacher taught all of the core subjects (reading, writing and arithmetic), music, physical education and had lunch and recess duty. No support staff or planning periods. Get the picture?

My walking and talking earned me the privilege of having my desk off in a corner away from the other children. Now you may be thinking, "that was cruel." It was kind of embarrassing and the teasing from some of the other students led to many "meetings" in the cloak room. But, as I look back, it was really for my good. I received individualized instruction, tailor-made for my ability. After reading *On Cherry Street* (the 1st grade reading book) three times, I was allowed to join the 2nd grade reading and math groups. By the end of my first year of school, I had completed both 1st and 2nd grade work and was promoted to 3rd grade. I thank

Mrs. Gladys Wheeler for not labeling me a behavioral problem, but channeling my energy and challenging my ability. My children and students are indebted to this great lady.

Regardless of how it is done, nurture is a demonstration of love from those who are present and involved in your life. These expressions assure you that you are all right. Nurture makes you feel good, significant and secure.

Getting the right kind of nurture—the right amount at the right time—can be difficult. It takes a lot of time and effort. Have you gotten enough nurture? Consider these four things as you reflect on your experience.

1. *Who nurtured you?* Parents are the primary people to bring you up as a healthy, whole person. Were your parents, grandparents, aunts or uncles involved in bringing you up?

2. *What principles were used to nurture you?* There must be some non-negotiables that you live by—basic social skills. You need to know how to cooperate, be honest, fair, kind, considerate and trustworthy, to name just a few. You must learn the principle of submission to authority and respect for others, as well as for yourself. What is your reference point? What is the moral authority in your life based upon? Did you learn that there are consequences for all behavior or have you been left to decide for yourself what is right or wrong?

In our home, we have what we call "kitchen table." At 6:30 a.m. our family gathers around the kitchen table. It is not always received warmly (We have a couple of sleepy-heads.), but we are committed to spending this time together before we hurry out of our house. We discuss the schedules and concerns for the day. Because we don't know what we will face each day, it is important that we approach everyday with a proper mindset.

As parents, my husband and I are doing all that we can to

live responsible lives before our children, and we take seriously our responsibility of instructing them. We understand that attitudes are taught as well as caught.

Whatever else may be said about the home, it is the bottom line of life, the anvil upon which attitudes and convictions are hammered out. It is the place where life's bills come due, the single most influential force in our earthly existence...It is at home, among family members, that we come to terms with circumstances. It is here life makes up its mind.

CHARLES SWINDOLL

3. *How were you nurtured?* Each of us has a unique temperament. We are all "one of a kind." Are you aware of your prevailing emotional tone? Your unique personality, gifts and aspirations should determine how you are motivated and disciplined. As far as you know, were these considered when you were being brought up?

4. *Where were you nurtured?* Home is the best of all possible places for this to occur. Unfortunately, in homes all across America, in the city and in the country, among Blacks, Whites, Asians, Latinos and others, many young people are growing up without enough nurture. Lack of love, unfair comparisons, unrealistic expectations, attitudes of helplessness, substance abuse, divorce, distant fathers and detached mothers contribute to forms of family dysfunction. Young people are at high risk of developing behavioral problems with such deficiency. Deficiencies are then acted out in the personality through attention-getting negative behavior and disagreeable attitudes.

Having said all this, I hope you see the connection between your nurture and your nature (attitude). You may not have asked for all that has happened to you or all that you're going through right now. But you are responsible for how you respond. You are in charge of your own attitude. It is really the only thing you have complete control over. Only you can change you!

Are you lacking in some areas? Do you need some "corrective emotional experiences" to make up for the deficits in your personality? If you feel shortchanged in the nurture department, a loving friend or relative can provide you with some of what you are lacking. There are people who love you and would love to show you that love. You must come clean though, admit that you need help, and be willing to receive the help that is offered. While you can't go to your parents and demand that they make up the difference, there are some things you can do.

Step 1. Get serious about your education. Set your goals. Dream big. Write out your vision and work toward bringing it into reality. Seek advice from people in the professions that you are interested in. Volunteer to get experience. Use the resources at your school and libraries.

Step 2. Get involved. Find an area where you can use and develop your gifts and talents by serving others. Get involved in the Girls and Boys Clubs and the YWCA and YMCA. Find some youth programs in your community.

Step 3. Share what you learn with someone else. Whenever you are healed or freed from a bad attitude or habit, use your experience to encourage someone else.

Questions

1. Has anyone talked to you about your attitude lately?

2. How do you handle a situation when an adult wants to talk to you about something that you know you need to talk about, but you still don't want to talk about it?

3. How do you feel your nurture can affect your attitude?

4. How do you like to be nurtured?

5. What one thing did your parents do to make you feel nurtured or loved?

6. What women have been the principal builders of your character and confidence?

7. Do you keep a scrapbook of awards, pictures of good times and notes of encouragement?

8. Do you understand your unique temperament?

9. Do you see the connection between your nurture and your attitude?

10. Are you aware of any areas where you have not been properly nurtured?

11. What are you doing to assist you in your recovery from any deficiencies?

12. How healthy is your attitude?

Mother Wit

What I most remember was an abiding sense of comfort and security. I got plenty of mothering, not only from Pop and my brothers and sisters when they were home, but from the whole of our close-knit community. PAUL ROBESON

And so our mothers and grandmothers have, more often than not anonymously, handed on the creative spark, the seed of the flower they themselves never hoped to see—or like a sealed letter they could not plainly read. ALICE WALKER

My mother told me I was capable of doing anything. "Be ambitious," she said. "Jump at de sun."
ZORA NEALE HURSTON

Each person grows not only by her own talents and development of her inner beliefs, but also by what she receives from the persons around her. IRIS HABERLI

When we, as youngsters, would accuse our mother of picking on us, her wise reply was, "All you'll get from strangers is surface pleasantry or indifference. Only someone who loves you will criticize you." JUDITH CRIST

My father always told me that I was the best. That there was no one better than me. Being able to define myself is something I attribute to my father and his "positive arrogance." CHARLAYNE HUNTER-GAULT

You are the product of the love and affection of your parents, and throughout your life you have drawn strength and hope from that love and security. NELSON MANDELA

Children respond to the expectations of their environment.
William Grier and Price Cobb

3
Siblings: Brothers and Sisters
(concerning brotherly and sisterly love)

Have you ever played a game called "The Telephone" where you sit in a circle and one person whispers a message in the next person's ear? Then that person whispers what she thinks she heard into the ear of the person next to her. This continues all the way around the circle. When the last person tells what she heard, nine times out of ten, the message is not even close to the original. In a situation among friends playing a game, this is usually harmless and funny. But in a family among brothers and sisters, even the slightest misinterpretation of what a parent intends can lead to hurtful feelings and cause fights. And sibling rivalry is no laughing matter.

You've probably wondered how children from the same family, with the same mother, in the same living environment, sharing the same bacteria, eating the same food and hearing the same conversation, can think and act so very differently. You are not the only one. Behavioral scientists have conducted extensive research on the similarities between siblings only to conclude that siblings growing up together are more different than they are alike. You or I could have told them that and saved a lot of time and research dollars. As the fifth of seven children and the mother of four, I know first-hand how different fruit can fall from the same tree. If you have brothers and sisters, you know I am right about it.

Members of the same family don't have the same experience just because they share the same house. Each of us starts out and stays different in major ways. We each have a way about us. At birth, this is apparent. Whatever happens in a home gets filtered through the lens of each individual's perspective. We see things differently, and often have different feelings about the things that happen. Our unique personality has to be considered when trying to understand our perspective.

I have a friend who grew up poor as far as this world's goods are concerned. His father was a hard worker and kept a job, but because he wasn't educated or skilled in any trade, his employment choices were limited to unskilled labor (i.e. janitorial work, lawn services, etc.). This standard of living really impacted this son, who was embarrassed, angry and ashamed. He was so resentful about what he didn't have, he wasn't able to really appreciate what he did have. He grew up blessed and didn't even know it. He had a two-parent family; brothers and sisters who loved him; a mother who prayed for him; and a father who went to work everyday, earned an honest wage and provided him with food, shelter and clothing. To this day, as a grown, middle-aged, middle-class man, he still gets angry and upset when his family gets together and someone starts laughing and talking about how 'po' (poor) they used to be. Other family members are able to look back and be thankful for how they got over. Not this brother. To him, growing up was painful and anything painful is not funny, but should be forgotten. This has been a source of some distance and more than one rift among these siblings.

As I said before, I am the fifth of seven children. I have two brothers and two sisters older than me and two brothers younger than me. We were born in three sets over a span of nearly 20 years. I was in the middle set. Needless to say, I experienced a very different mother than my older sisters and my youngest brother. If you have siblings 5 to 7 years older than you, you've probably heard that you "get away with murder" or "Mama ain't raising you like she raised us." If you're an older sibling, you have probably said the same thing to them. I know I have heard it and I have said it. And it is partly true.

When my older siblings were coming up, my mother was a young woman—fiery, quick-tongued and quick-tempered. When I came along there were five children, and she had mellowed out somewhat. By the time my youngest brother arrived, she was tired. Even though we experienced her at different times in her life, there are a lot of common threads that link our experience with Mama.

The greatest gift that my Mother gave to my siblings and me was a sense of ourselves—who we were, our individuality and her appreciation of it. She did an excellent job of making each of us feel as if we were her favorite child. She never compared us to one another and refused to allow anyone else to. On more than one occasion she "got somebody told" for making a comparison between us or asking why one couldn't be like another. If we felt slighted, it wasn't because we were, it was because we chose to feel that way. There may have been times when one of us wanted to be like another one. I remember wanting to be studious and athletic like my brothers or a cheerleader like my sister, but I don't ever remember my mother suggesting it. I can still hear her say, "Be your self. Don't ever want to be somebody else. You can't be anybody else, so don't even try."

There was only one thing that she required that my siblings

35

and I do alike. She insisted that we put each other (sisters and brothers) before others and that we prefer each other over others. I remember complaining once about not having any friends or anybody to play with. Her response was a classic: "You don't need any friends. You have each other. Play with your brothers. That's why I had all of you in the first place." Or my grandmother saying, " Don't go looking for trouble. Don't go and start a fight. But if you see your brothers or sisters in a fight, remember whose side you're on. We'll figure out who was right and who was wrong when you get home." They were concerned that we love one another.

I believe that the one thing that I did that hurt my mother the most was when I fought and argued with my younger brother. She would ask us, "out of all the people in the world to fight, why do you want to fight each other?" It didn't matter to her who had started it. No reason was good enough. She would "tear us both up" for fighting and make us make up (apologize and tell each other we loved each other) afterwards. I would fight him at home and defend him in the street. Most of my childhood fights were for one of two reasons: somebody either talked about my Mama or somebody picked on my younger brother. I learned to be loyal at home. Now that I have children, I understand the pain that she felt when she saw us fighting with one another.

I grew up in a home at a time when family mattered. Your brothers and your sisters were your best friends. You were expected to support and look out for one another. When one did well, you all did well. When one was struggling, you all were struggling. While I had forms of dysfunction in my family, sibling rivalry was not one of them. Now that we have all grown up, have our own families and live in various parts of the country, our fellowship is not as frequent or as intimate as it could be. But that's on us. Our relationships are healthy. My mother and grandmother made sure of that.

What about you? How healthy are your relationships with your siblings? Do you feel that your parents treated you differently, but equally? Mothers and fathers try to love and rear their children equally, but in reality they are not always successful. It is a known fact that it is easier to raise a child whose personality is similar to yours. More than one child adds its own challenge, not to mention a child with a strong-willed, don't-tell-me-anything temperament. Ideally, parents should raise their children equally, but differently, considering each unique personality. To use the same approach with children who have different temperaments would be a disservice.

There are so many things to consider when you are trying to understand relationships, especially between brothers and sisters. If you feel that you have been slighted by your parents, and this is affecting your relationships with your siblings, try to put some objectivity into your perspective. Consider these facts.

Fact 1. Parents are human and will make mistakes. They are people too. They are not perfect. They can hurt your feelings and not even know it. They don't mean any harm, they just don't know. At times, they may say or do something out of frustration, anger or ignorance that will hurt your feelings. Forgive them.

Fact 2. Parenting is a skill that you acquire. You understand it better by and by. Some skills are gained by trial and error. Parenting is definitely an on-the-job-training profession. The only way that some parents know how to raise their children is how they themselves were raised. (Maybe an auntie or grandma can give you some perspective on your parents' childhood). Gather some facts about how your parents grew up. Be understanding of them.

37

Fact 3. Parents have issues—problems and situations that you had nothing to do with. You may remind your mother of your father or vice-versa. There may be some unresolved conflict between them. You become the target of the misdirected anger.

Fact 4. You and your siblings are different. If your parents have been paying attention, they know this. Try and understand that it is your parents' responsibility to train each of you up in the way you should go (differently), but equally (accomplish the same result). Appreciate them for it.

Fact 5. Everyone has strengths and everyone has weaknesses. Don't be envious and jealous of your siblings' accomplishments. Jealousy will kill your potential, misdirect your attention and paralyze your effectiveness.

Fact 6. You will disagree with your brothers and sisters in this lifetime. They will make you so mad. Don't stay mad with them. Deal with the problem. Don't attack the person, focus on the issue. Let your brother or sister know in no uncertain terms how you were offended. (You are miffed that they ruined your blouse, wore your new outfit before you did, used your last of whatever it was or embarrassed you trying to impress somebody.) Get it out. Regardless of how well or how long they defend their position, keep the conversation focused on the offense and don't get personal. Even if they don't ask for forgiveness, forgive them and tell them that you want to move on.

Fact 7. Every family needs a peacemaker. Decide to be a peacemaker in the family you were born into and in the family you create. If there are strained relationships, become the sacrifice (yield your rights and set aside your pride) and initiate some dialogue. You have nothing to lose, but a brother or sister to gain.

Questions

1. Do you have a good relationship with your brother(s) and sister(s)?

2. Have you analyzed why your relationship is good or bad?

3. Are you holding a grudge against them for anything?

4. When was the last time you forgave or were forgiven by another family member?

5. Is there anything that you get upset about when your family gets together and discusses the past or present?

6. What is the greatest gift your mom has given you?

7. Is sibling rivalry a major issue in your home?

8. Which of the seven "facts about parents" has helped you the most?

9. When you disagree with a sibling, do you attack their personhood by calling them names?

10. Are you willing to be the peacemaker in your family?

11. What do you think the author means when she says that different fruit can fall from the same tree?

Mother Wit

For there is no friend like a sister—In calm or stormy weather; To cheer one on the tedious way, To fetch one if one goes astray, To lift one if one totters down, To strengthen whilst one stands. CHRISTINA ROSSETTI

He is a fool who treats his brother worse than a stranger. NIGERIAN PROVERB

The hatred of relatives is the most violent. TACITUS

Accidents will occur in the best-regulated families. CHARLES DICKENS

The greatest thing in family life is to take a hint when a hint is intended—and not to take a hint when a hint isn't intended. ROBERT FROST

The family is one of nature's masterpieces. GEORGE SANTAYANA

"I can forgive but I cannot forget" is only another way of saying, "I cannot forgive." HENRY WARD BEECHER

Forgiveness is the key to action and freedom. HANNA ARENDT

We flatter those we scarcely know, We please the fleeting guest, And deal full many a thoughtless blow to those who love us best. ELLA WHEELER WILCOX

4
Your Neighborhood
(a place of amazing grace)

If I asked you where you're from and for directions on how to get there, you would have no trouble telling me. You could probably give me several routes to your neighborhood, complete with landmarks and all. You know your physical geography—how to locate yourself by neighborhood, street, city, county, state, country, and even continent. But how aware are you of your historical geography? Do you know that where you're from, the people you grew up with and the mindset of your community have influenced who you are? Where you are from—your 'hood (neighborhood) has impacted your personality. In this chapter, I will share "the lovely days" in my neighborhood and how they impacted me.

It doesn't matter where you're from, a person usually has a certain amount of pride associated with where they grew up. I have traveled halfway around the world, sung on 5 of the 7 continents, performed before governors, magistrates, officials and potentates, and the same question always comes up—*where are you from?* I get great pleasure from telling people where I'm from and that something good can come out of a small town of seeming unimportance.

I was raised in a small town up south with a population of

less than 2,000, better known as Mount Hope, West Virginia, where there was just about one of everything. One stoplight. One Post Office. One Grocery store. One Filling station. One Hardware store. One Bank. One ABC (Alcoholic Beverage Company) or liquor store. One Doctor's office. One Jail. These establishments were open to everyone. And then there were some places that were segregated by practice, although there were no signs posted to that effect. One such place was the funeral home. We traveled to Beckley (nine miles south) or Greentown (six miles north) for our funeral arrangements. Other places were the churches. What Dr. Martin Luther King, Jr. said about the 11 o'clock hour on Sunday mornings being the most segregated hour in America was certainly true in Mount Hope. In the city limits, there were four large churches that whites attended and three churches where blacks worshipped. Main Street ran east to west from one end of town to the other, lined on both sides with most of the businesses and churches. What wasn't on Main Street was one block to the north or south of it.

I am told that back in the day Mount Hope enjoyed its share of notoriety. My father-in-law told me of his escapades to Mount Hope on many a Friday and Saturday night. With coal mining being the major industry of the state, this small town was booming when mining in the area was active. But when I was growing up, the mine was a filled-in hole in the side of a hill, the company store was closed and the city was on the verge of becoming a sleeper.

Just as there were segregated places for worship (churches) and for woe (bereavement), housing was pretty segregated as well. There were three major neighborhoods where most blacks lived: MacDonald Hill (off the By-Pass); the Stadium Terrace (North Pax Avenue, a.k.a. subsidized housing or the projects) and Kessler's Holler (North Virginia Avenue). There were some blacks that lived downtown, but most lived in one of these three places. At various times, I lived in all three.

From as far back as I can remember up to around age 7, I lived between two houses on MacDonald Hill. My mother and grandmother lived close to one another and we children did a lot of going back and forth between the two houses. I must have spent most of my time at my mother's because that's the one I remember most vividly.

It was a small house with five rooms, four of which we used—a bedroom, a kitchen, a front/living room and a bath room. There was also a fifth room, which didn't have any heat in it and was appropriately called the "cold room," which we primarily used for storing things.

Houses weren't lined neatly in a row on MacDonald Hill. Each house was sort of off to itself, so it wasn't a planned neighborhood in the conventional sense, but it was a number of houses linked together by dirt paths. I remember traveling only one other dirt path besides the one to Gramps' house during my early years. My mother didn't believe in "wearing out your welcome" with a lot of visiting from house to house. When I asked if I could go over to *so and so's* house she would say, "You have a house. You can stay home. I know what's going on here," implying that she didn't know what was going on over there. I experienced what my children call "lock-down" first hand. And I'm glad about it.

As I look back, living on MacDonald Hill when I did was a real blessing. It was a controlled, sheltered environment in which to develop my internal value system, convictions and personality. It is believed that 85% of your personality is developed by age 6. It was good for me not to have a lot of outside influences. Unaware of it at the time, I adopted this same practice with my own children. One of my students brought this to my attention. This is another example of how your orientation is connected to your present behavior.

My family's move from MacDonald Hill gave me many opportunities to outwardly express what I had worked in as my inner values and convictions.

When I was about 7 or 8, we moved to the 'Hood, the Stadium Terrace. The Stadium Terrace was the subsidized housing project of Mount Hope. Thirty-five, two-family row houses numbering from 1 - 70 were home to 69 families. It was segregated housing, separated by a stretch of road between numbers 1-49, which were for white families, and numbers 51-70, which were for black families. Number 50 was the rental office.

The Stadium Terrace was a neighborhood complete with front yards, a centralized playground, parking lot and street address. I lived at 51 North Pax Avenue with my mother and some of my siblings. My grandmother and other siblings lived at 63 North Pax Avenue. Just like before, we lived between the two residences.

We children amused ourselves on the playground, jumping rope and shooting marbles, playing baseball, basketball, as well as other games such as *Red Rover, Red light/Green light* and *A, My Name* (I'll come back to that one later). We rode our bikes on the sidewalk and drew lines in the alleys for *Kicktop* and *Hop Scotch*. Grown-ups sat under their side windows and watched our talent shows—some burning rags to keep the mosquitoes and flies away, a few eating Argo starch, and all encouraging us with much applause.

The Stadium Terrace was a pretty stable neighborhood with not too much coming and going. Most of the children graduated from high school, some attended college, some went into the military and others moved to the city with older siblings or relatives. The *great exodus* of families came as a result of Black Lung settlements by the United Mine Workers Association to retired coal miners. With these lump sums of money and monthly pensions, families could afford to buy homes. (Our move to Kessler's Holler was a result of my stepfather's settlement.)

All in all it was a decent place to live—a simple, yet satisfying neighborhood where everyone knew everyone else. I had many opportunities to show what I was made of. Every fight I ever had, I had in the Stadium Terrace. I also met my childhood best friend, Donna, there. While no one but my mother ever disciplined me, there was someone who told on me if I was ever out of line. There were a few colorful characters in the Stadium, but for the most part, it was a caring community, where everyone wanted good for the children—a place of amazing grace. I spent my Elementary through early High School years growing up there.

The Stadium Terrace was the neighborhood I grew up in. It served me well. I survived it and to some extent thrived there. It was not posh, but there was pride among the people. We cut our lawns, planted flowers and decorated for the holidays. I lived in the projects but the projects didn't live in me. We were poor economically, but not impoverished spiritually or morally. Where do you reside on the inside? I was raised in a housing project, but I didn't have any intentions of living there as an adult. This leads me to explain the *A, My Name* game. The lyrics went like this:

A, my name is Ashley, (or any name beginning with the letter A) My husband's name is Alan. We come from Atlanta, And we sell apples.

And so forth through the alphabet in this fashion. Inherent in this game that we played day in and day out was a determination to do better with our future. We were expected to do better. I can't remember anyone ever saying

S, my name is Susan.

45

My husband's name is Sam.
We come from the Stadium.

We saw ourselves living somewhere else. The games we play tell a lot about our goals and aspirations. How do you see yourself? Where do you see yourself ten years from now? What are your goals, dreams, aspirations and visions?

I had dreams and visions with plans and methods to reach them. Education was my way to get there. It was and has always been important in the Black community. It is the surest and safest way to reach your goals. What do you need to accomplish your goals? What are you doing now to get there? Regardless of what you're told, there is no quick way to success. No matter where you're from, you can go where you want to go. Accomplishment starts with a dream and comes by perseverance, commitment and hard work. Get started!

Questions

1. Can you describe your neighborhood as well as the author described her neighborhood?

2. To what degree do you feel that you currently understand your neighborhood and its impact on you?

3. Are there any famous people who have come from your neighborhood?

4. Do you have a sense of pride about your home and neighborhood?

5. Where do you see yourself 10 years from now? What are your dreams and aspirations?

6. What do you think the author means by the phrase "internal value system?"

7. Do you think young girls today can have a determination about their futures?

8. What steps have you already taken to secure your future success?

9. Have you allowed anyone to evaluate your future plans?

10. Do you believe that regardless of your circumstances, you can go where you want to go?

11. If your family has been stuck in a cycle of poverty for a few generations, do you want to be the one to break that cycle?

Mother Wit

I have always known that being very poor, which we were, had nothing to do with lovingness or familyness or character or any of that . . . We were quite clear that what we had didn't have anything to do with what we were.
LUCILLE CLIFTON

My philosophy of life is that if we make up our mind what we are going to make of our lives, then work hard toward that goal, we never lose—somehow we win out. RONALD REAGAN

Shallow men believe in luck ... strong men believe in cause and effect. RALPH WALDO EMERSON

Nothing in the world can take the place of persistence. Talent will not; nothing is more common than unsuccessful men of talent. Genius will not... the world is full of educated derelicts. The slogan "Press on" has solved and always will solve the problems of the human race.
ATTRIBUTED TO CALVIN COOLIDGE

For me, education means to inspire people to live more abundantly, to learn to begin with life as they find it and make it better. CARTER WOODSON

The best way to fight poverty is with a weapon loaded with ambition. SEPTIMA CLARK

It isn't where you came from: it's where you're going that counts. ELLA FITZGERALD

5
Dealing with Deficiencies
(filling life's voids)

My first car was a brand new 1979 Datsun 310GX. It was beautiful—a 5-speed, (standard transmission) black hatchback with dark red interior. It was a great car. It was a faithful car. I drove it and two of my brothers, my husband, my sister-in-law and my brother-in-law drove it. It was still running when we gave it away. Dotty (affectionately called) and I shared many wonderful experiences together. There was one experience that I'll never forget.

It was a Sunday afternoon and I was on my way home from church service. I was driving on the highway approaching a ramp. As I passed the ramp I checked my rear view and side mirrors for oncoming cars. I saw none, so I proceeded to change into the right lane. The next thing I knew, I heard tires rubbing together. I had collided with a Datsun 280ZX (Girl, it was sharp!!!). Fortunately, there was no damage to either car. This experience changed my driving habits. Since then, I turn and look over my shoulder in addition to looking in the mirrors to make sure nothing is coming. I had just learned about a driver's blind spot in an up close and very personal way.

A blind spot is an area where vision is hindered or

obscured. The 280ZX was in my blind spot when I checked my mirrors, therefore I didn't see it. A blind spot can also be a deficiency that a person is not aware that they have. Just as the driver of a vehicle operates with a handicap or blind spot, every human being operates with deficiencies. Deficiencies are not always easy to recognize because we have been living with them for most, if not all, of our lives. We are too familiar with them. Others can see them, but we can't. Some of us have learned how to compensate for areas of deficiency. We learn how to get by without the things that should be present in our lives. You may be thinking *I've been getting along just fine up to now,* and *what I don't know won't hurt me.* But that's not true. What you don't know may hurt you. Ignorance is not bliss! Others of us live with voids in our lives, barely getting by, and spend lots of energy trying to secure what is missing. The best thing to do is to recognize the deficiency and deal with it.

Life is complicated enough by those things that you already recognize. By dealing with your known areas of deficiency, you will gain a definite edge and advantage in life. These suggestions are intended to protect you from encountering and colliding with blind spots—those deficiencies that you may not be aware of. Take a look at the following list. It is not complete, but it does include some things that may not have been in your life, but should have been.

Ten Areas of Deficiency:

1. You grew up without your father in the home.
2. You grew up without your mother in the home.
3. You grew up without a father-figure in the home.
4. You grew up without a mother-figure in the home.
5. You grew up where your being accepted was based upon your performance.

6. You grew up in a home where love was not expressed (no hugs, kisses, etc.).
7. You grew up in a home where you were made to feel inferior, dumb and stupid.
8. You grew up in a home where you were made to feel superior and better than others.
9. You grew up in a home where you were never encouraged and nurtured.
10. You grew up in a home where you were stifled and not allowed to express yourself.

Does any of these circumstances describe your situation? If you answered yes to any of these, you have recognized some deficiencies. Recognition is the first step towards filling life's voids—you must know that they exist. Then you can do something about them. I came to recognize an area of deficiency in my life at a marriage retreat. The speaker made the following statement:

"If you grew up in a home without a father, you have a deficit in your life. And you need to deal with that."

I had heard this statement declared with passion and force many times before, (my husband was the speaker) and I must admit that for most of those times I felt offended. I was offended, not only because it insisted that I was lacking something, but also because I knew many girls who grew up *with* fathers and have a whole lot of problems. I reasoned that if they turned out as they did with fathers, I hadn't turned out so badly growing up without a father in the home. While I believe that it is best to grow up in a two-parent family with both your mother and father, I also know that you can make it with one good parent present. I never challenged the speaker for his conviction. I felt that he was entitled to his opinion. But inside, I grappled with it. I became defensive.

Finally, I decided to stop just hearing him and really listen to what he was saying. When I really listened to this statement, I mean, with my guard down, I understood it and was able to receive it. I had set up inner dialogue (self-talk) as my defense mechanism to deal with this area of deficiency. I told myself that every situation is different. (I knew some instances where it would have been better if there were no father present than to suffer with a dysfunctional one). The first thing to remember when trying to deal with deficiencies is:

Don't become defensive.

I realized that my defensive posture was a form of denial. I was in denial about the fact that I had missed out on something because I didn't grow up with a father in my home during my formative years. I turned out all right because my mother, by the grace of God, had done double duty, but I had missed not having an earthly father. There were things that I didn't enjoy—those daddy-daughter things—because I didn't have my father in my home.

I've known my father all of my life. We lived in the same town. I call him daddy and I love him, but the truth of the matter is, he was not a daddy to me when I was coming up. He was my father. I never did any daddy-daughter stuff with him. I don't remember ever sitting on his lap. He didn't teach me how to drive or to understand sports. He never screened my dates or boyfriends. He took me to the only baseball games I ever attended, and paid for some things that I needed for various activities I was involved in, but I never enjoyed having him present in my life on a daily basis. I didn't know him as a provider and a protector. I see how my girls just love their time with their daddy and I realize that I never had the benefit of that relationship when I was their ages. Their father is their provider and their protector. He has their back at all times. He's crazy about them and they know it quite well. The second thing to remember when dealing with deficiencies is:

Don't live in denial.

There are many things that you learn about men when you grow up with a father in your home. You learn about providers and protectors when your father is present. You learn about male and female differences. You see that men and women think differently; they reason differently; and they come to conclusions very differently. You also learn different forms of communication. For example, women say a lot by saying a lot, while men say a lot by saying little.

Fortunately, when I was growing up there were wonderful men in my life who filled my daddy-deficit. They compensated for my voids. My brothers, uncles and my grandfather were the principal male players. I was blessed to have brothers who complimented me and protected me. I love and admire my brothers. I have great memories with all of them. My brother, Matthew, served as a brother/father to me. He brought me candy for Valentine's Day, always told me that I was pretty and gave me his last when we were in college together. My brother Cuther, who is younger than I, also felt the need to look after me. I remember that when I was planning my wedding, he asked me if I needed anything. I am blessed to have the brothers I have. The third thing to remember as you address areas of deficiency is:

Deal honestly with your deficiencies.

I am not angry about growing up without my father in my home. I accept it as a fact of my life. That is just the way it was. But thanks be to God, I enjoy a wonderful relationship with my father now as an adult. We enjoy one another and I am grateful for this. I have a relationship with my father because I realized that even as an adult, I wanted a relationship with him. I needed a relationship with him. He needed a relationship with me. And his grandchildren should have a relationship with him. For many years I prayed for my father. I have always wanted the best for his life. I recognize that my willingness to work to keep our communication going and to build a relationship with him was part of the answer to my prayer. We have a good relationship because I can forgive what wasn't done and should have been done on my behalf, and be grateful about the good that has occurred.

I recognized an area of deficiency in my life, and I dealt with it. While the blood was still running in both of our bodies, I took the opportunity to fill one of my life's voids. I followed the three steps that I suggested to you. I stopped being defensive. I stopped denying my deficiency. And I dealt honestly with my deficiency. Be encouraged to deal with your deficiencies. You will be so glad that you did.

Questions

1. Are you aware of any blind spots in your life?

2. Did you find yourself in the "Ten Areas of Deficiency" list? If so, was it painful seeing yourself there?

3. What do you tell yourself about your deficiencies? How honest are you with yourself?

5. Are you maturing in the way you are dealing with your deficiencies? (One indicator of a maturing personality is the desire to find deficiencies and deal with them.)

6. Why does the author say that deficiencies are not always easily recognizable?

7. Who sees your blind spots most easily, you or others?

8. How do you feel you are dealing with your deficiencies? Are you compensating?__ Getting by?__ Barely getting by?__

9. In your opinion, what is the difference between a "Daddy" and a "Father"?

10. Of the three steps that the author suggests, which step do you struggle with the most?

11. What plan do you have to deal with your deficiencies?

Mother Wit

Whatever reason you have for not being somebody, there's somebody who had that same problem and overcame it.
BARBARA REYNOLDS

If you want to truly understand something, try to change it.
KURT LEWIS

What do we live for, if it is not to make life less difficult for each other? GEORGE ELIOT

The triumph song of life would lose its melody without the minor keys. MARY MCLEOD BETHUNE

Start where you are with what you have, knowing that what you have is plenty enough. BOOKER T. WASHINGTON

The most lonely place in the world is the human heart when love is absent. SADIE ALEXANDER

If you let conditions stop you from working, they'll always stop you. JAMES T. FARRELL

Being defeated is often a temporary condition. Giving up is what makes it permanent. MARILYN VOS SAVANT

My friend and mentor, Fred Smith, taught me this truth: If I can't do something about a problem, it's not a problem; it's a fact of life. JOHN MAXWELL

6
Interrupting a Dysfunctional Life-Cycle
(right living as a way of life)

In the back or along the side of just about every garment you own, there is at least one tag, and sometimes two. On the tag is the brand name with its logo, the size, type of fabric, where the garment was assembled and how to care for it. For example, the tag on my son Jonathan's new FUBU jersey says:

FUBU THE COLLECTION XL
MADE IN KOREA
CARE OVER
When you flip the tag, it continues with
100% POLYESTER HAND WASH SMOOTHLY OR
MACHINE WASH SEPARATELY IN LUKE WARM
WATER ONLY NON-CHLORINE BLEACH TUMBLE
DRY LOW OR HAND DRY REMOVE PROMPTLY
KEEP IRON OFF DESIGN COOL IRON

With all of these instructions on how to properly care for this jersey, I'd say that it definitely falls into the delicate garment category. Although the tag suggests that it can be machine washed, I would not risk it on the normal setting. Jonathan says that he plans to have it dry cleaned. But, we'll see how long he wants to spend his money doing that. It's new now and he's all excited about it. But when the new smell fades and the funds are low, we'll see if it makes its way to the dry cleaners or to the kitchen sink.

When I was coming up (in the old days), I used to hand wash a garment like this. Nowadays, with all of the technology and modern advances there is little need to hand wash anything. My washer has a delicate wash setting that is as gentle as hand washing. If my son does take a chance at machine washing his jersey (and I know he will at some point), I will suggest to him the most delicate wash setting. To further insure that no damage is done to his 'gear', he should interrupt the most vigorous part of the wash—the spin cycle, remove the jersey and air or line dry it.

While this jersey is a nice garment and needs certain consideration to keep it that way, my washer is not a respecter of garments. (It does the same thing in every cycle, no matter what kind of clothing is being washed.) Once it starts, it goes through its various cycles unless it is deliberately and intentionally interrupted. The key to saving this jersey from damage is to carefully follow the instructions and interrupt the vigorous spin cycle. Just as there are procedures to follow to preserve my son's FUBU jersey, there are principles to follow for success in life. I've seen young people take better care of their clothes than of their character. They sport live rags, but live ragged lives. Why do you think that is? I have found it to be a mentality thing, and it all goes back to orientation—(how you were raised), and follows through to your perception (what has been put in your mind), self-talk (what you say to yourself) and behavior (how you act things out). You have been impacted in ways that you are not even aware of.

Your orientation—(the way you were raised)—has affected your opinions, beliefs, attitudes and behavior. If a check came to your house on the 1st or 3rd of every month without anybody going to work to earn it, you have been impacted. If you have witnessed people trading Food Stamps for cash to buy items that Food Stamps aren't supposed to buy (such as alcohol, cigarettes, etc.), you have been influenced. If you have been told "that to get over is what you have to do to get ahead, that you have to beat 'the man'—that's the way it is, and everybody does it," you have been affected. If you have been a part of any of this or been where there is domestic violence, you have been a part of a negative cycle. Well, I am here to tell you that that's not the way it has to be and that everybody doesn't have to do it. I'm not telling you what I've read or what I've heard. I'm telling you what I know.

I've been caught in a negative cycle before. Alcoholism was a form of dysfunction that I grew up with. It was pervasive—family members and people in the community drank as a means of dealing with disappointment, as a form of escape and as a social entertaining pastime. But I knew I didn't have to. I knew I could adopt productive coping strategies (reading, praying, meditating) and positive pastimes (sports, music, etc.). I know that any dysfunctional, negative cycle can be interrupted. I realize that the dysfunction that comes as a result of the negative-cycle has great momentum. Throughout society, it is spinning out of control.

It is going to take a deliberate act on your part to interrupt the cycle. To do nothing will almost guarantee a repeat performance in your life of some of the dysfunction that you grew up with. By an act of your will and a fight against the path of least resistance, you can break the negative cycle.

Negativity is not a respecter of persons. It will influence anybody's behavior. The only explanation for some behavior is a negative attitude. A stinky attitude by any other name is still a stinky attitude. Being pleasant, whether it is accepted or not is the best attitude to have. Remember this, right is right even if no one does it, and wrong is wrong even if everyone does it.

If your mama, grandmama, aunties, cousins and friends all had children before marriage, became welfare mothers, didn't finish high school or get their GED, it doesn't mean you have to do the same thing. You can break the cycle by deciding to live right and to do right.   Learn from the mistakes of their past, don't live them out in your life. Entering womanhood as a healthy, whole person, with a minimum amount of dysfunctional baggage is your goal. You have one destination, but there are two routes—the way that seems right and the way that is right. The way that seems right is wider than the way that is right. You may have identified some patterns of dysfunction that have been passed down your family line, such as alcoholism, substance abuse, promiscuity, lying, deceit, laziness, irresponsibility, and so on.

If you recognize that you have picked up some of these attitudes and patterns of behavior, you can interrupt this dangerous course with a deliberate choice—the way of right living. You are not destined to perpetuate the dysfunction of your parents or your peers.

There are many principles that lead to a successful life. When they are adhered to, you will prosper and be successful. They are like promises that you can bank on. You may be thinking that you don't know any of these success principles. My guess is that you may already know some of the ones I will share with you. One is often called the "Golden Rule," and it goes like this: "So in everything, do to others what you would have them do to you." (Sometimes it is misquoted as, "do unto others before they do unto you.") Another example of something you've probably heard is, "you reap what you sow." I believe that I have heard it on a number of movies.

It is usually rendered with a negative connotation or meaning behind it, but it doesn't have to be negative. If you sow good seed, you will bring forth a good harvest. But whether it is delivered in a negative way or positive way, it is more than just a clever saying. It is a true fact of life. It is a law of the universe.

Here are some principles that I have heard and that have helped me.

1. Start where you are, use what you have, do what you can.
2. Do what you have to do, when you have to do it, regardless of how you feel.
3. If you want something done, strive for it and get the job done yourself.
4. The dictionary is the only place where success comes before work.
5. Never forget that hard work and diligence will help you defeat any negative aspect that life sends your way.

Before we go any further, let me clarify what I mean by success. I do not mean an accumulation of stuff, although there is nothing wrong with material wealth that has been honestly acquired. Real success is not measured by what kind of house you live in, or what car you drive—in short, success is not what you possess, but what possesses you. I've read about millionaires and billionaires who are miserable. They can buy anything that money can buy, but aren't happy. And then I know some people who are very successful—living very rewarding, fulfilling, lives, and don't have or need a lot of money to do it. These people are committed to causes larger than themselves. They are making a difference in the lives of others. They are literally pouring themselves out for the benefit of others, and their service and sacrifice is paying off. They may not have six or seven figure salaries, but they have an inner peace and contentment that truly surpasses all understanding. They have found the secret to success.

What cause are you committed to? For what are you willing to deny yourself and delay your gratification? If you haven't identified a cause yet, you and your future are good ones to start with. If you have ever wondered, "what is the secret to people's success?" wonder no more. There really is no big secret. Successful people are using success principles. If you want to achieve success and prosper, start with the success principles I have shared with you and consider how you can apply them to your life everyday. Now that you know better, I'm expecting you to do better!

Questions

1. Do you hand wash your delicate clothes or dry clean them?

2. Do you take better care of your clothes than you do your character?

3. Have you analyzed what has been put in your mind?

4. Do you monitor what you say to yourself?

5. Do you regularly monitor how you act out the thoughts that go through your mind?

6. What do you do when you have a pleasant attitude and people reject you?

7. Have you identified any patterns of dysfunction that have been passed down your family line?

8. What will it take to interrupt a negative cycle?

9. The principle: "You reap what you sow" is often used in a negative context. What is the alternate application of this principle?

10. Are you committed to a cause larger than yourself?

11. Have you shared with anyone the causes that you are committed to?

12. At this point in the study, are you still examining your orientation?

Mother Wit

A life of reaction is a life of slavery, intellectually and spiritually. One must fight for a life of action, not reaction. RITA MAE BROWN

Change is not made without inconvenience, even from worse to better. RICHARD HOOKER

Children learn first and best from their families. Just as by the end of the second year their language is that of the people with whom they live, so their behavior is stamped with the seal of their adult protector. SADIE GINSBERG

Practicing the Golden Rule is not a sacrifice, it's an investment. BYLLE AVERY

No life will ever be great until it is dedicated and disciplined. PETER C. B. BYRNOE

The most important thing a father can do for his children is to love their mother. THEORORE HESBURGH

There are no illegitimate children—only illegitimate parents. LEON R. YANKWICH

The hardest job kids face today is learning good manners without seeing any. FRED ASTAIRE

Children have more need of models than critics. JOSEPH JOUBERT

Part II

Soul Food
(Your Mental and Emotional Diet)

Do I believe I'm blessed? Of course, I do! In the first place, my mother told me so, many, many, times, and when she did it was always quietly, confidently. . . . and I know that anything she told me was true.

Duke Ellington

7
How You See Yourself
(the way you think)

Y ou may not realize it, but what you believe others think about you and how you think about yourself can be traced to the experiences you had as a child and the emotions you attached to those experiences. Whatever you felt, saw, heard or otherwise perceived while you were coming up, found a place in your memory. Whether it is in your conscious memory or subconscious memory depends on the experience, but your perceptions are stored in one of the two places and are easily accessed.

When I was coming up I perceived that some people wondered whether or not my siblings and I would make something of ourselves. My perception was not based on a single experience or event, but rather on a feeling I had. I don't remember hearing much talk about it. But as we all know, people communicate in verbal and nonverbal ways. And silence on an issue can speak much louder than words.

I could *feel* the unasked question, *"What will those kids make of themselves?"* Their doubt was based on what they saw with the naked eye. They didn't know what was taking place inside of our home (what I shared in Part I). Those who doubted could only see a family who would be considered at-risk today: a family that was on welfare, receiving commodities, a single parent household. They didn't see a family that would come up through a difficult way—a discouraging way at times—but where hearts would become tender and compassionate because they knew what sacrifice was all about. They knew what humility was all about. These children felt the stigma of illegitimacy and would develop compassion, commitment, love, resolve and determination to live godly lives and fulfill their purpose. Those who doubted just didn't know.

My perception regarding the unasked question had some merit. After graduating from high school, college and the university and achieving a measure of success as a professor, conductor and international performing artist, I returned home for a concert performance. Following the performance, one of my teachers from junior high school came to me and with tears in her eyes and a quiver in her voice, said, *"We didn't know. We just didn't know."* It was an awkward moment for me. Here was a teacher that I respected and had taught me well, who was admitting that she and others never expected such accomplishment from me. I remember trying to lighten the moment by saying, "That's okay, not many knew. God and my mother were the only ones who really knew for sure."

Perception is powerful. What we think others think about us can greatly influence what we think about ourselves. Therefore, our perceptions cannot go unchecked, but must be inspected. Not all perceptions based on past experiences serve us well in the present. How was your perception of yourself formed? How is your perception serving you? Does your perception block you in any way? Does it motivate your behavior positively? What are you doing to overcome any blocks that hinder you?

Much of who we are depends on how we think others will

respond to us. Our personality comes out in interpersonal relationships—whether one-to-one or in a large group setting. We say that we don't care what others think about us, but in truth, we place ourselves somewhere on a social ladder. We wonder at times if we're important or not. After all, we are social beings. In addition to getting ahead, we want to get along. Our consciousness is full of questions like, "What should I do?" "How will people react to me?" "Who should I be?" Have you ever had those questions before?

My perception of what some others thought of my ability didn't discourage me. It could have, but instead, I found a challenge and courage in it. And I've always enjoyed a challenge. *"Challenge me, I'll show you,"* has been my motto. I learned it from my mother. Her motto was simply, *"Watch me."*

In my case, I had received enough nurture and affirmation at home to guard me from depositing negativity in my spirit. I had no excuse for not excelling. I was always expected to do my best! Nothing more and nothing less. My mother said that I was somebody and would do great things. Her words counted because she knew me and loved me. She was important to me. So in my mind, what she said was so. To this day, when things get hard and I wonder how I'll get through, I can hear my mother say, *"You can do it."* I call upon her daily in my mind for a good word. She has spoken words of encouragement to me many times while I've been writing this book. I remember our talks together.

There were others too. Let me add that there have always been people in my life who have encouraged and helped me. I encourage you to rely on your resources—a parent, a coach, sponsor, anyone who believes in you and builds you up.

No one can escape from the challenge of life and our perception of it. The negative, ugly opinions of others may be a theme with a number of variations that you have to deal with throughout life. It may be hard at times—a fight, a struggle even, but the fight will make you strong.

I'm so grateful that I learned how to fight while I was growing up. What I mean is—I learned how to hold on through tough times. I learned to keep going. I didn't understand why I had to experience the difficulty I faced, but I knew that anything worth having was worth fighting for. I persevered, was strong, had confidence and overcame obstacles. If I had not fought my way through those discouraging times, I would have never enjoyed the good that was awaiting me. Let me encourage you to fight a good fight, work hard and persevere. You will survive the difficult stages. Learn how to get fuel out of whatever fire you are in. Be diligent, be faithful and you'll be moved to higher places.

What about you? Have you ever had someone doubt your ability, or not wish you well? It may never be spoken, but you get the feeling that's what others are really thinking. What do you do with those feelings or perceptions?

First of all, determine if your perception is true. Bring it out in the open and shine the light of awareness on it. Admit to yourself that you are having these thoughts. But be careful to hold them up against the truth of the matter. Sometimes the way you see a matter is not the complete truth. Try to find an objective perspective. An older, wiser relative, counselor or friend may be able to help you examine the facts and work truth in your perception. Then you have two options:

1. You can use your perception as inspiration and motivate yourself to reach your full potential; or
2. You can agree with another person's assessment of you and fulfill their prophecy concerning you.

What will you do? Let me encourage you to use every opportunity to reach your full potential, to exceed expectations, to beat the odds, to go against the grain. Rise to any occasion and do whatever needs to be done. Reframe what you perceive to be negative in others' thinking towards you—make it a challenge. See yourself as someone who acts. Visualize yourself doing that which you desire to do. That's how it all started for me.

I used to see myself doing what I do now—teaching and performing. I watched whatever music shows came on TV. (*The Wizard of Oz, The Sound of Music, The Lawrence Welk Show, Shirley Temple,* etc. We didn't have BET when I was a child.) I would sit and dream of being a performer. I sang songs from the radio. My mother provided the background vocals, while I sang lead. I practiced and performed day in and day out in front of family, friends, whoever would listen. At the close of the school year, I would set up school in my front yard, teaching anyone who would come. I saw myself then as I am now—a musician and a professor.

Imagination is powerful. I continue to use my imagination even as an adult. Every major concert hall I've performed in as a professional artist, I imagined myself there beforehand. I used to dream of singing at Carnegie Hall in New York City. I had many opportunities to attend performances there during visits to the Big Apple, but I wanted my first time in the theater to be when I was on the stage performing. My dream became reality. In November of 1990, I walked in front of Carnegie Hall to see my name in the marquee box, proceeded to a dressing room with my name on the door, and at concert time, walked out on the stage as a soloist.

Early on, I identified my gifts, then seized every opportunity to perfect the talents I've been given. My ability is a combination of both innate ability and learned skill. Not that I have arrived by any stretch of the imagination. I have survived and thrived. I am good at what I do because I work hard at it.

You are gifted also. Reaching your goals and fulfilling your purpose depends upon you seeing yourself do it. It would be nice if others saw it with you, but if no one ever shares your vision, or gets behind you and encourages you, you have the power within your own perception to make it happen. How do you see yourself? Do you see yourself as a grasshopper or a giant? Are you unable or well-able? It's how *you* see yourself that really matters. Go for it!

Look To the Future

They said I couldn't,
But I thought I could,
They said I shouldn't,
I believed I would.

I knew who I was
And what I wanted to be.
They felt I didn't,
But I'd make them see.

It didn't come easy.
Tough times, I agree,
But I was determined
To be the best of me.

Many years have since passed,
And they smile, they're so proud.
But I believed in myself
And just look at me now!
VERA R. CHITTY

Questions

1. The author mentions two types of memory. Do you know what conscious memory is? Do you know what subconscious memory is?

2. What unasked questions do you feel others have about you? Why?

3. Do you feel that others see you as "at-risk" or destined for success?

4. What have you gone through that enables you to have compassion for others?

5. Do you feel there is a stigma that you are working to overcome?

6. How is your perception serving you? Is it your friend or foe?

7. Do you enjoy a challenge? What is your motto when it comes to facing challenges?

8. Are you strong enough not to deposit negativity in your mind?

9. What people serve as the positive voices in your life?

10. Have you learned how to use hard times to make you tougher?

11. What positive things do you visualize yourself doing?

Mother Wit

Listen carefully to what the country people call mother wit. In those homely sayings are couched the collective wisdom of generations.   MAYA ANGELOU

All that you accomplish or fail to accomplish in life is a direct result of the images you hold in your mind.
HORTENSE CANADY

No one can make you feel inferior without your consent.
ELEANOR ROOSEVELT

The delights of self-discovery are always available.
GAIL SHEEHY

We usually see things not as they are but as we are.
LOUISE BEAVERS

Everybody in the world is seeking happiness—and there is one sure way to find it. That is by controlling your thoughts. Happiness doesn't depend on outward conditions. It depends on inner conditions. It isn't what you have or who you are or where you are or what you are doing that makes you happy or unhappy. It is what you think about it.   DALE CARNEGIE

No one can figure out your worth but you.   PEARL BAILEY

Your mind is what makes everything else work.
KAREEM ABDUL-JABBAR

8
What You Say to Yourself
(your self-talk)

Have you ever heard the following expression?

Sticks and stones
may break my bones,
but words can never hurt me.

I grew up hearing this and at times, even said it. If you are unfamiliar with it, just ask an older sibling. I'm sure they'll tell you that they've heard it before. I am told by my youngest daughter, Charity, that it is still in use today. She reports that many at her school say it now.

This little saying is usually declared immediately after someone has suffered some verbal abuse. It has a nice lilting rhythm and a cute little rhyme, but its message is not at all true. Though it seems quite innocent at first hearing, it contains some serious error. It might be one of the biggest lies we've ever told! If words can never hurt us, then why are we so concerned and upset about what is said about us?

The truth is that words can hurt us. Sticks and stones break us down on the outside, but hard, harsh, hateful words break us down on the inside. The bruises we incur from a fall can be easily bandaged and patched up, but internal bleeding is serious business. Words have the capacity to damage us on the inside—to bruise our spirits and damage our emotions. It may take years before we realize the extent of the damage.

My physical fighting career, which lasted for about five good years (from age 7 to about 12), was launched because I felt I had to defend myself against verbal attacks. I can remember only a few of my bouts that were for reasons other than words or what somebody said. Words do hurt and they hurt badly.

Words are powerful. They penetrate deep down inside of us. They lodge in our minds and form fully-illustrated pictures that conjure up all kinds of images, feelings and fears. Subconsciously, we comment to ourselves on what others have said to us and have not said, and on what we have done and left undone. This subconscious conversation with ourselves is what is referred to as self-talk. If you have ever repeated the opening expression, *"sticks and stones..."* or any other expression to yourself in your mind, you have engaged in self-talk.

It is reported that we are able to talk with our mouths approximately 150 to 200 words per minute, and can speak with our minds at a rate of about 1300 words per minute. Imagine that! We can speak with our minds over six times as many words per minute as we can speak with our mouths! Now that's doing some serious talking! What in the world are we saying to ourselves at that rate? How healthy are the conversations that we are having? Are they building us up, or are they bringing us down? I am sorry to say that unfortunately, a very high percentage of what we say to ourselves is negative. Most of our inner dialogues are amplified, screaming, self-defeating negative thoughts. Why is that?

Why do we speak so ugly to ourselves? Well, the

unfortunate reason is that we have been spoken to in ugly ways. We have internalized what people near and dear to us have said and done to us. Regardless of whether the assault was intentional or not, the abuse has damaged our self stuff (esteem, worth and confidence), taken up residence in our spirits and to a large degree controls how we communicate with ourselves and others.

We process our experiences. If during our early experiences we are emotionally and physically damaged, we devise defense systems—whether right or wrong, adaptive or damaging—for dealing with such situations in the future. We use these rules for protection against future hurt, and we keep on playing by them. We don't always remember the details of hurtful events, but we definitely remember our emotional reaction to the events. We also remember how we dealt with it at the time, and when placed in a similar situation, we will act the same way again.

Deep down in the recesses of our minds are experiences with emotions attached to them that await their opportunity to come forth. These emotions only need a subliminal cue or signal in order to become activated. Self-talk often serves as that cue. What you say to yourself affects how you feel. Therefore, it is imperative that we monitor what we say to ourselves and not let our thoughts run rampant.

What do you say to yourself after you have failed at something? If you beat up on yourself with negative comments like *"I can't do anything" or "I am pitiful,"* you'll end up feeling that way. But if you encourage yourself by admitting the error or shortcoming and determine to learn from it—*"I missed the mark this time, but I won't miss it every time,"* you'll feel encouraged to try again. Realize your feelings don't always tell the truth, but you can straighten out your feelings by fixing your self-talk.

Some pretty ugly things have been said to me in my

lifetime. I have been called out of my name in some interesting and unmentionable ways. I have been called everything but a child of God. But I am thankful that the negativity did not stick with me and become a part of my life. I refused to believe it and refused to repeat it to myself. I admit it hurt and it hurt badly, but I learned early how to talk to myself, how to comfort myself. I remember saying to myself, *"I hear what is being said to me, but I don't agree with it."* I also vowed that if I ever had children, I would not curse at them. I had no control over what was said, but I had complete control over the way I reacted to it. My reaction and response was my last word!

Let me encourage you to have the last word concerning yourself. And make it a very good word. It won't happen overnight. It takes time. Where you are now and the damage that has been inflicted upon you didn't happen overnight. It was a process and recovering from it is a process.

I am told that it takes a minimum of 21 days in order for a new behavior to become a habit. So for the next 21 days I want for you to do the *"Positive Talk"* exercise. You will need notecards, a pen and a journal. This exercise is to be done at the start of your day and at the close of your day. Follow the steps below:

Day 1
Step 1. Meditate on positive statements. Fix your thoughts on what is true, good and right. Think about things that are pure and lovely, and dwell on the fine, good things in life, yourself and others. Some positive statements to get you going include:

      1. I like myself.
      2. I am not ashamed of where I come from.
      3. I like my appearance.
      4. I can make things happen for good.

5. I'm proud of my family.
6. I have potential.
7. I am gifted.
8. Today is the best day for me to do what I need to do.

Step 2. Write these positive thoughts on eight notecards. Keep a copy of the thoughts with you at all times so that you can refer to them often and place the other copies in places where you will see them regularly (on the bathroom mirror, on your desk, in your purse, etc.).

Step 3. Stand in front of a mirror and read the thoughts to yourself.

Step 4. Look at yourself and be thankful for at least one thing that is true and good, right, pure and lovely.

Step 5. Write down in your journal everything that you are thankful for before you go to bed.

Day 2 through 21, repeat Steps 3, 4, and 5.

If you have suffered from verbal abuse—being cursed, criticized and ostracized, you will need to do some reparenting. You need to say positive, esteem-building statements to yourself. Just as any negative self-talk is a result of conditioning and reinforcement, you can change your self-talk into positive affirmations with some motivation, reinforcement and encouragement. Focus on the enjoyable aspects of life and yourself. Commend yourself on who you are, what you do well and what is wonderful about life and living. Every day, say something good to yourself about yourself. Adopt the language of a believer and achiever.

Replace any negative self-talk such as *I can't do anything* and *I'll never be anything* with positive, empowering thoughts such as *I can do anything I put my mind to* and *nothing is impossible. Things might be difficult I may even struggle, but I have what it takes to accomplish what I work for.*

You can encode yourself and your experiences so that you have a positive mind-set as your point of reference. Be patient with yourself. Take all of the time necessary to repair and restore yourself. You're worth it. Don't just take my word for it. Look at those around you who have tried this approach and have been successful. Successful people realize that they are also valuable people. Now that you have a healthy perspective concerning how you should talk to yourself, you have the standard by which to separate the truth from the lie in what others have planted in your spirit and what you are saying to yourself. Throw out the lie and deposit the truth that you can do anything in your heart.

Not every comment and experience is going to be a pleasant one for you. Life is made of things that are chosen and things that are unchosen. But when criticism is hurled and negativity unfurled toward you, and the language degenerates to an unacceptable level, you don't have to adjust your self-talk to the downward spiral. Root out the negative influences and monitor what you say to yourself. You *can* have the last word with yourself. And it can be a good word. You can't control the remarks, but you can compose your response to the remarks—both your outer and inner response. In this life, you cannot afford to have one negative conversation with yourself!

Questions

1. When was the last time you were in a fight? Who started it?

2. Do you feel that words can hurt you?

3. According to the author, where do harsh, hurtful words break us down?

4. If words addressed to you are not true, what should you do?

5. If words directed to you are true, what should you do?

6. What do you say to yourself when someone attacks you verbally?

7. Do you feel that you must defend yourself when you are attacked verbally?

8. Are you aware of your defense systems?

9. The subconscious conversation we have with ourselves is referred to as_____.

10. Does your self-talk build you up or tear you down?

11. Is there any area of life where you have accepted a negative self-view of yourself?

Mother Wit

Positive anything is better than negative nothing.
LORRAINE HANSBERRY

Advances are made by those with at least a touch of irrational confidence in what they can do.
JOAN L. CURCIO

Poor self-image is the number one problem for women. And it is the Indian's biggest problem and that of teenagers too. It used to be my biggest problem until the day I suddenly decided that I don't care if I impress people or not because if I make friends with people I don't need to impress them.
PRINCESS PALE MOON

You don't make progress by standing on the sidelines, whimpering and complaining. You make progress by implementing ideas. SHIRLEY CHISHOLM

Perspective is worth 80 I.Q. points. ALAN KAY

I've always believed no matter how many shots I miss, I'm going to make the next one. ISIAH THOMAS

In the darkest moments I can still find peace.
MARIAN ANDERSON

Most folks are about as happy as they make up their minds to be. ABRAHAM LINCOLN

9
Why You Do The Things You Do
(your behavior)

When I was coming up, a young lady didn't just leave the house whenever she felt like it. She made sure someone knew that she was going out, where she was going, who she'd be with and when she would be back. In my case that someone was my mother. Before I left to go anywhere, I made sure that I told her my whereabouts. Inevitably, I mean almost always and without fail, I would be told at least one of three things (and sometimes all three). "Act like you got some sense," "Remember who you are," and "Don't be acting a fool." My mother gave me these admonitions before I went public.

If you've never heard these phrases before I'm sure you've heard something similar. These phrases had special meaning in my community. Implied in these words is the desire that you think before you act. My mother and others knew and understood that if they could get us to take the time to think, we would probably act appropriately. They realized that all behavior begins in the mind and wanted to make sure that we engaged our minds before saying or doing anything.

This memory from my adolescent years is alive and well.

It is a functional memory, that is, it does something for me. I am keeping this part of my upbringing alive in the way I am raising my own children. I find myself telling them the same things I was told. You have functional memories too. What are you keeping alive and well through your behavior?

My husband reinforces this teaching with an abbreviated version that has changed over the years. He started out clearly making his point with flailing arm gestures, contorted facial expressions and a higher than normal pitched voice stating, "Remember, Daddy wants you to THINK." It has been modified to a one-word admonition, "THINK!" and even further to one gesture—pointing his index finger to his head. The children all realize that any request to go anywhere will be accompanied by my admonitions or his routine. They are so conditioned that before he gets the chance to go through his ritual, they usually stop him and say, "Dad, I know, you want me to THINK!"

What about you? Do you think before you act? Or do you just go on with your bad self and try to figure it out as you go along? Let me encourage you to think through your behavior BEFORE you act. What I mean is, consider all possible consequences that will follow anything you do. Be willing to suffer the consequences of your decisions and actions. I guarantee that if you take time to fully weigh the consequences of your behavior before the fact, you'll be glad that you did.

All behavior is motivated by our thought processes. Rev. B.J. Tatum often says, "You act the way you act because you think the way you think." And he is all the way right about it. It is for this reason that we opened Part II of this book with a discussion on how we construct reality—our perception and self-talk. How we see ourselves and what we say to ourselves affect our emotions and motivation. It is hard to change undesirable behavior if we focus only on the behavior. We must address what is behind the behavior.

Much of what we do day in and day out is out of habit—we don't consciously think about it. For example, we unconsciously breathe, swallow, blink, and clear our throats. Only when we think about something do we behave consciously. But when we don't activate our conscious mode, which is most of the time, our subconscious goals and motives are in charge. These buried motives (our subconscious) influence what we do.

You are probably thinking, "I think before I act." And I agree that sometimes you do. But I would venture to say that most of the time your behavior is a reproduction of what you grew up with, what you have seen and what you think will work for you.

Our present behavior is influenced by our past, particularly our childhood. Take cleaning the kitchen as an example. I grew up hearing that the kitchen should be the cleanest room in the house because that is where you eat. To this day, I try to keep my kitchen clean. I follow the same procedure that my mother used, from the order of cleaning (table, then counters), to the washing of dishes (silverware first, then glasses, cups, plates, bowls, containers and lastly pots, pans and skillets). I realize that there are many ways to clean a kitchen, but I do it the way I grew up watching my mother do it. Remember our discussion on orientation? Orientation controls a large amount of your current behavior.

This is not difficult to understand. It doesn't take a rocket scientist to figure out that if we come up where healthy, positive behavior is modeled, we are likely to imitate healthy, positive behavior. If unhealthy behavior is modeled when we come up, then we are likely to display unhealthy behavior. Language is a clear example of how behavior is modeled. If you grow up in a home or community where bad language is not disdained but is the order of the day (it's accepted), you are more likely to use this kind of language too.

It is very important that you go back and as best as you can, trace the path you took to get to where you are behaviorally. What behaviors can you trace to what you saw coming up? What behaviors are a result of how you see things (your perspective)? What behaviors are a result of what you tell your self (your self-talk)? What's in you is bound to come out. Know why you do what you do.

Our perceptions and self-talk must come under truthful scrutiny, because every fruit of behavior begins as a root of belief. Whatever spin we place on things works its way out through what we say and eventually ends up influencing what we do. Most, if not all of our actions begin as attitudes. You know I'm right about it. How many times have you been reprimanded and your mother asks, "What were you thinking?" She knew your action started as an attitude.

People act out for a number of reasons. There are so many influences on behavior—educational status, racism, poverty, neighborhood, economic disparity between the haves and the have nots, backlash of the civil rights movement and affirmative action legislation, unemployment, and the list goes on and on. Behavioral disorders, along with poor academic performance, top the list as the main reasons why many children are referred to the counselor's office. In reality, these two concerns are closely related if not one in the same—disruptive behavior is a symptom of low self-esteem caused by poor academic performance. When we don't feel good about ourselves we are tempted to give up—we feel we have nothing to lose.

Have you ever heard the phrase, *"There is a place and time for everything, and this is neither the time nor the place?"* I remember hearing this whenever someone was behaving inappropriately. There is acceptable and unacceptable behavior. Some behavior is acceptable but inappropriate in certain settings. You must learn to discern what is appropriate in different situations. Cultural values influence our behavior. For example, some kids develop coping styles in the 'hood in order to survive that don't transfer or work very well for success in mainstream society. Cuttin' up (talking loud, laughing and generally having a good time with your girlfriends) is acceptable behavior at a football game, bonfire or picnic out in the open air, but is inappropriate behavior for the library, movie theater or school assembly. You must respect community space. Don't get me wrong. I love to have a good time with my girlfriends. But you cannot violate someone else's rights in order to exercise your rights. Remember there's a time and place for everything.

People also act out to receive attention. You know the adage "the squeaky wheel gets the grease." Some girls think that it is more profitable to act a fool. Their behavior is an informed choice that has been reinforced by good results. They think, "If I act out, I'll get some attention." And they are right. Remember, I said before that some people feel that attention from negative behavior is better than no attention at all.

We all have to decide whether we will behave by compulsion or by choice. We don't mind making choices when we understand the benefits—when we see the value and meaning behind them. For many young ladies, the attention and affection that they receive from negative behavior feels a lot better than the loneliness and isolation they feel when they don't bring attention to themselves. The return on the negative behavior is worth it to many. That is why it so important to have a good understanding of what we tell ourselves. Be a young lady who through hard work and delayed gratification is committed to reaching her full potential.

Historically, close knit families have leaned on pillars that

87

have provided strength and stability for their communities—religion and the church, the extended family and kinfolk, family members helping out where needed (no set roles) and a good education. These four values are deterrents to poor behavior. Belonging to a group and being responsible for representing it well has served as a type of restraint. I remember hearing often, "Remember who you belong to, whose name you carry." I had a name to uphold and a legacy to protect. The home has been and always will be the best place for home training. When this breaks down, other places like churches, civic groups, clubs, etc. may offer help.

People who tolerate and accept inappropriate language and behavior from you do not have your best interest in mind. As my kids used to say "They not your friends." Anyone who condones (overlooks) your self-destructive behavior is not being compassionate. People who really love you expect the best from you even if you have to go through some growing pains to get there. Beware of people who have low expectations of you. *Remember, they not your friends.*

You may be thinking, "I don't want to act so differently—like I'm from a different planet or something." I feel you. Your struggle is an old one. For centuries, young people have had to choose between safe behavior and at-risk behavior. The temptation to join the wild crowd with its thoughts and behavior is pressing you. Guard your behavior! Many people have an agenda for you that is not in your best interest. Do not allow them to squeeze you into their mold or way of thinking and acting.

Behavior is more than what you see a person do. There are emotional and psychological dimensions that influence what we choose to do. Right behavior will follow if your thinking is right. If you are practicing the *"Positive Talk"* exercise of Chapter 8, then you are off to a really good start toward good behavior.

Questions

1. Do you leave the house when you feel like it?

2. Who gives you a lecture (admonitions) when you go out of the house? If the answer is no one, are you prepared to do the mature thing and lecture (admonish) yourself?

3. Are you a person who will do anything or do you think of the consequences of your actions before you act?

4. The author's mother realized that behavior begins where?

5. Do you realize that you will one day tell your children many of the things you have been told as an adolescent?

6. Can you determine what appropriate behavior is and act appropriately?

7. Do you exhibit negative behavior to get attention? Do you feel that attention from negative behavior is better than no attention at all?

8. Have you decided to think and act beyond your immediate circumstances and aspire to reach your full potential through hard work and delayed gratification? What does "delayed gratification" mean?

9. Do you represent your family name well?

10. Do you know who are *not your friends*?

Mother Wit

For a long time the only time I felt beautiful—in the sense of being complete as a woman, as a human being—was when I was singing. LEONTYNE PRICE

The character of even a child can be known by the way he acts—whether what he does is pure and right.
KING SOLOMON

For as he thinketh in his heart, so is he. KING SOLOMON

Ideas won't keep: something must be done about them.
ALFRED NORTH WHITEHEAD

I have always thought the actions of men [and women] were the best interpreters of their thoughts. JOHN LOCKE

Fear is not a wall but an emotion. And like all emotions, it can be overcome. GWEN GOLDSBY GRANT

Few things are harder to put up with than the annoyance of a good example. MARK TWAIN

Live so that you can at least get the benefit of the doubt.
KEN HUBBARD

When a man learns to understand and control his own behavior as well as he is learning to understand and control the behavior of crop plants and domestic animals, he may be justified in believing that he has become civilized.
E .C. STAKMAN

10
Recovering from Rejection
(healing your feelings)

When my children were growing up, they experienced their share of fumbles and falls, and then some. Following each episode they would come in crying and making a big to-do. Sometimes there were obvious signs that they had been hurt (cuts, scrapes, bruises, blood, etc.). These incidents were easy to comfort and care for. A little hydrogen peroxide, a lot of blowing on the area and a Band-Aid was usually about all that it took to make them feel better. When they were very young, they felt even better if their Dad or I fussed at whatever they had fallen on, and told it not to do that to them again. You probably remember this from your upbringing as well. And then there were other times when the damage was less obvious. No outside indicators—no blood, no bruise, no broken skin.

When pressed to tell where it hurt, they had a very hard time finding the exact location. They couldn't pinpoint where it hurt, they just knew that it hurt. And they wanted some relief. Their Dad and I usually met this challenge by kissing everything in the entire vicinity to try and make it better. Just doing something gave them some relief and they usually returned to their activities. Have you ever had a pain that you couldn't quite locate? I mean, you hurt— you felt the gnawing on the inside, but couldn't quite describe where. It seemed as if every spot you pointed to was not quite right. You just couldn't get a grip on it. Take heart, you are not alone. I know what you mean and how you feel, for I have had my share of hurt on the inside.

The hurt on the inside sometimes comes as a result of someone finding you unworthy, not measuring up to his or her standard, or simply rejecting you. Rejection is a bitter pill to swallow. You may tell yourself "forget them" or "I don't need that," but it is still painful. Rejection is so difficult to take because we were not created to receive rejection. It is a foreign agent that seeks to invade our being. We can take ridicule, reprimand and rebuke, but rejection penetrates our core. One particular incident is particularly memorable to me. I can still remember the pain and sting I felt from being rejected.

It was my third year in college. I had been part of a gospel choir and had made many friends. We hung out together and for the most part, I enjoyed spending time with them. We shared a lot of fun times—traveling, singing and just having a good time. At the end of the year, there was talk among those that I felt especially close to about forming a gospel group—starting a music ministry. I heard about it, but I never really was in on the real conversations. I never asked much about it. My mother always told me to stay out of other people's business. "They will tell you what they want you to know," she would say. I heeded her advice and didn't inquire. I figured they would tell me about it sooner or later.

Well, the talk continued, the plans were made and the group was formed. My sooner or later never came. They never talked to me about it. They didn't invite me to be a part of it. I was not included in the group. I don't know if I was even considered. I felt rejected. I was very hurt. Here I had spent years with these people who I thought were my friends, and now they had excluded me. I continued to be cordial and everything, but I was really hurt by their decision. Fortunately, I had a good friend who encouraged and comforted me when I was feeling down and out. I'm glad I had her in my life. Well, the so-called ministry fizzled out, following by some degree of scandal and suspicion and I was really glad that I hadn't been a part of it. But I must admit that I was very hurt by the rejection of not being asked to be a part of it in the beginning.

There have been other instances when I have felt pain on the inside. I have felt like there was a hole in my heart at times. Not in the physical heart organ, but in my soul-heart, at the seat of my emotions. I couldn't really describe it then as I can't adequately now, but the pain was very real. It hurt on the feeling level. When you hurt on the inside, a hug and a kiss may make you feel better at that moment. You need that, but you need much more in order for healing to take place on the inside.

Hurts on the inside come from pain inflicted on you from someone significant in your life—a parent, a relative or a trusted friend. In many cases, the cause of your pain is from some form of abuse. You may not even recognize that you are being abused, because it is not always aggressive. Abuse can be very subtle and slick. Abuse from anyone—family, friends or foes, can be very devastating and damaging. It is so pervasive, affecting you at many different levels. You are probably very aware of the active, physical types of abuse where there is violence, assault and battery; the sexual type, where there is incest and molestation; and verbal abuse, where you are damaged by words used on and against you. Verbal abuse is not necessarily illegal like physical and sexual abuse, but it is just as destructive. When you've been yelled at, blamed and shamed and told you will never amount to anything, you have suffered from verbal abuse.

You can also be abused in subtle and silent ways. The silent, passive types of abuse are of a more emotional, feeling nature. If someone withholds affection and love from you, that is a form of emotional abuse. Emotional abuse is also when someone tries to control you by manipulating you. You may be told "If you loved me, you would do this or that," or "If you tell anybody, nobody will believe you." And then there is what is called emotional incest, where a parent switches roles with you. You start to act like the parent, while they act like the child. A parent may confide in you as a substitute for the other parent. They share all of the problems of the marriage and/or challenges of work with you. And if you don't agree with it, affection is withheld from you. This is unhealthy and unfair to you.

All forms of abuse are damaging to you. All abuse hurts you. It might hurt on the outside, inside, or both. But you can be healed from the hurts. You can recover. It requires a decision and some work. It is not pleasant. In many cases, the guilt, shame and embarrassment that kept us from saying anything about it when it occurred, will try to keep us silent when we try to deal with it. You will feel pain, anger, bitterness and a whole range of emotions. You may have to go way down before you can come back up. But your healing is worth the journey.

The journey toward healing your feelings requires some open, honest admissions. It demands the truth, the whole truth and nothing but the truth. Here are some steps you can take to get your journey started:

1. Find someone you can trust to confide in. Reconstruct the event. (Retell what happened). Deal with the pain you feel. What is the real deal (truth) about how you were hurt?

If you are angry, admit it. Don't deny your true feelings. Express them.

2. Examine your current relationships. Beware of being attracted to abusive, dysfunctional people. Don't repeat the mistakes of the past.

3. If you lost your virginity because of incest or molestation, grieve the loss. Cry and do whatever you need to do to get out your pain and anger. Be patient with yourself.

4. Realize that you are not to blame for the abuse you have suffered. You were taken advantage of and it was not your fault. You are not to blame!!!

5. Decide to move on ahead with your life. You are an overcomer. You can't change what has happened, but you can distance yourself from it.

6. Reparent yourself. If your parents are out to lunch, maybe some caring adults can serve as substitute parents who will nurture your spirit back to wholeness.

7. Keep a journal of your progress. Refer to it often. Congratulate yourself when you are doing well. Encourage yourself in the areas where you need to be strengthened. Stay at it. Adolescence, that time when you are most vulnerable, is usually the time when pain on the inside first surfaces. I have been there in my own life, besides living through this critical time vicariously with two of my daughters and my son. It has not been easy—seeing the pain they experience from being ridiculed, isolated, talked about at school and in the community. I feel their pain but can't do much to alleviate it.

They have to work through it. Each handles it differently. Two internalize it and take a while before letting it go, while another one talks about it, cries through the recall and gets it up, out in the open and out of the system.

We each have different tolerances for pain. I have a very high tolerance for pain, whereas my husband and two of my children have a very low tolerance for pain. Those with low tolerance want relief—quick, fast and in a hurry. And those of us with high tolerance tend to suffer a lot longer. Let me encourage you to decide not to tolerate the pain of past hurts, rejection and abuse. Start to deal with it now. The healing of your feelings is a process. There is no quick fix. But as long as you are honestly dealing with your areas of hurt, you are making great progress. Stay at it. Fight a good fight, keep the faith, finish your passage!

Questions

1. Are you hurting on the inside right now?

2. So far in your life, how have you handled the hurts on the inside?

3. Have you been rejected lately?

4. What memory of rejection do you carry that is very painful?

5. When you are rejected, where do you look for an answer to the question: "Why was I rejected?"

6. Do you have a good friend who encourages you when you need it? Do you have an older wise friend who can give you wisdom and encouragement when you need it?

7. Has a boy ever rejected you for another girl?

8. Does a good hug help when you hurt on the inside?

9. Are you aware of any active physical types of abuse that you have suffered? If yes, what are your doing to heal from it?

10. From the 7 steps that promote healing, which step is most relevant for you?

11. Are you prepared to reparent yourself wherever you see the need to do so?

12. Is there a quick fix available to heal the pains of the past?

Mother Wit

Believe in yourself and your abilities. There are lots of other folks who'll tell you, "It can't be done." JASMINE GUY

No one can make you feel inferior without your consent. ELEANOR ROOSEVELT

There is in this world no such force as the force of a man determined to rise. The human soul cannot be permanently chained. W. E. B. DUBOIS

Why hate when you could spend your time doing other things? MIRIAM MAKEBA

And a good rejection slip can be more educational than a mediocre workshop. ANONYMOUS

The greatest success is successful self-acceptance. BEN SWEET

No one can figure out your worth but you. PEARL BAILEY

Many people know how to criticize, but few know how to praise. ETHEL WATERS

I refused to be discouraged, for neither God nor man could use a discouraged soul. MARY MCLEOD BETHUNE

Forgive, forget, and move on. LOUIS SULLIVAN

11
Dreaming Dreams Into Reality
(seeing what you believe)

Among the most famous speeches ever delivered is the one given by Rev. Dr. Martin Luther King, Jr. in Washington, D.C. in 1963. It is known as the *I have a dream* speech. While some don't consider it the best speech he ever delivered in terms of tone and substance, it is recognized as a true masterpiece. It is powerful. People are moved to tears upon hearing it from film clips or whenever someone recites it.

It is said that the speech was rather impromptu. It was unplanned. It happened in the moment. John Lewis states in his book *Walking with the Wind: A Memoir of the Movement,* that as Dr. King moved toward his final words of his prepared text, he could sense that he was falling short. It was a good speech, but not nearly as powerful as many he had made before. Lewis writes, "he hadn't locked into that *power* he so often found. Mahalia Jackson, who was seated just behind King, leaned in as he was finishing and urged him out loud, "Tell them about the *dream*, Martin." The *dream*, one of Dr. King's favorite images, had been used before and was the perfect fit for this occasion. Responding to the importance of the moment, Dr. King delivered, *"I have a dream..."* The momentum was there.

Everything was just right. And the rest is history. A speech that could have fallen flat was inflated because he remembered his dream.

Dr. King's dream was his vision for America. He may have received it while asleep, but he was very much awake when he talked about it. It was a driving force in his life. He hadn't seen the things he dreamed of, but in his mind's eye, he could visualize them. What do you see with your mind's eye? How colorful and vivid is your imagination?

Dreaming has always been important to us. There is power in a dream. When we were younger, our elders often asked us *what are you going to be when you grow up?* We were encouraged to dream big, outlandish dreams. We were encouraged to shoot for the stars. The sky was the limit. We could dream to be doctors, lawyers, movie stars, scientists, businesswomen, whatever. There were no limits to our dreams. And my mother never stopped encouraging me to dream. I remember being home for a weekend just before my undergraduate graduation. My mother asked me what my plans were after graduation. I answered that I would like to go to Baltimore to Peabody Conservatory or to New York to attend Juilliard or the Manhattan School of Music. I told her that I would like to study at a conservatory and learn how to become a complete artist. She looked me dead in the eye and said, "Then, go. If that's what you think you need to do, then you should do it." I countered by saying that it was very expensive and that I didn't have any money. Her response was "you'll find a way. Have you asked them to give you money? Ask for what you need." She never stopped encouraging me to live out my dreams.

Well, I never attended those institutions, but I didn't let go of my dream. When I came to Illinois, I remembered to ask for money. I came as a Fellow to study to become a complete artist. As a Fellow, I received a tuition and fee waiver and a little money to live on. My Fellowship appointment was part of the fulfillment of my dream. There is a beautiful coffee table book entitled *I Dream a World*. It is a compilation of powerful photographs of women who lived out their dreams—performers, scholars, educators, etc. Their success began with their dreams—dreams that they were willing and committed to holding on to until they became their reality.

Do you have a dream? Who taught you how to dream? Are you criticized because you know where you're going? How does that criticism affect you? Keep your eyes on the prize. Hold on to your dream. It will come to pass.

Before going to bed, I usually tell my children to have sweet, blessed dreams. I remember hearing that or phrases like *sleep tight, don't let the bed-bugs bite* from my mother when I was a child. I want for them to have pleasant, restful sleep.

Most bed-time dreams occur spontaneously, much like the way Dr. King's famous speech happened. They are seldom really planned. We generally go to bed at night and depending upon how our day has gone, what we have on our minds or what we had to eat, we dream pleasant dreams or unpleasant ones. Sometimes we receive wonderful inspiration in a dream.

When I was a child, I was taught a simple bed-time prayer. You probably have heard it before. It goes like this:

> *Now I lay me down to sleep.*
> *I pray the Lord my soul to keep.*
> *If I should die before I wake,*
> *I pray the Lord my soul to take.*

At this point the prayer was usually personalized to include any requests I might have for myself and for others. It went something like this:

> *Bless Mama, bless Gramps,*

> *Bless all my sisters and brothers.*
> *Help me to be a good girl and*
> *Do the right things. Amen.*

Several years ago, I was teaching at a conference and I had the great opportunity to hear a missionary to Africa speak. He was a dynamic speaker. He shared how his dream of visiting the Motherland and ministering turned into a very extended stay and his life's work. At the close of his address he referred to the bed-time prayer, *Now I lay me down to sleep.* He heard his young daughter pray this prayer one night and get a few of the words mixed up. In her error, there is a great message for us. Listen up.

> *Now I lay me down to sleep.*
> *I pray the Lord my soul to keep.*
> *If I should wake before I die,*
> *I pray the Lord my soul to take.*

If I should wake before I die is where the message is. Are you awake before you die? We live at a time where there are a lot of people walking around asleep. How many people do you know are alive, but asleep? I know hundreds, maybe even thousands. They are walking around in a sleep-state.

No purpose, no vision for the present or future. No dreams. They just live from day to day. They have no goals. No aspirations. No energy towards accomplishment. Just asleep!! You hear it when they speak. You see it in their walk. When you ask them what do you want to be when you grow up? What do you see yourself doing in 5, 10, 15 years from now?, they shrug their shoulders and say "I don't know," or worse than that, "nothing." Why is it that with so many opportunities to do anything we can imagine we want to do, people can't tell you what they want to do? Where have all of the dreams gone?

We all have an arrival time (our birth) and a departure time (our death). We are to be productive in the in-between time. What are you doing with your in-between time? Our ancestors accomplished so much with so little with their in-between time. They had little money and little opportunity, but lots of hope and plenty of dreams. They used what they had and did what they could—built schools, invented things, made discoveries, and the list goes on and on. What did they have that your generation does not have? They had dreams. They had visions. They had goals. They had commitments to do whatever it took to make their dreams a reality. They did it for me and they did it for you. They are our history, our heritage and the shoulders upon which we stand. Our foreparents left so much for us to remember them by. What will our distinguishing mark be?

Dreams have always helped us along the way. Who gave us permission to stop dreaming? Why did we stop? Why is it that we have a whole generation that lives only for the present? What has happened? Do our lives fall short because we've forgotten how to dream? What has happened to our imaginations? Who stole our dreams?

Dreaming requires skipping out of yourself and looking ahead. It involves not being held or caught in your present circumstances and situations. You may be asking, "how do you start dreaming?" Use these few steps to get started.

Step 1. Write down what you like to do. It doesn't matter what it is. Write it down.

Step 2. Write down what you do well. List the gifts and talents you already have.

Step 3. Write down what needs to be done. Compare what you like to do and what you do well with what needs to be done. Use your gifts to fill the needs that exist.

Step 4. Research the career choice you've made. Find out all you can about it. Visualize yourself there. Make sure your self-talk is confident.

Step 5. Do all that you can to become excellent in where you are now, as a student, as an athlete, as a musician, etc. Excellence is transferable. You can take good habits with you from one career to another. Work as if your life depends on it. It really does.

Step 6. Work enthusiastically and diligently for the love of it. Never work for just money or prestige. Do what you do because you love it and want to do it. Do it because you are free to.

You need to set some short-term, mid-term, and long-term goals—where you want to be in 5, 10 and 20 years. Visualize yourself there and then work back to where you are now. Determine what you need to do in order to realize your dreams and goals. Look at what you're doing now and see how it is aiding your future. If your friends are going nowhere fast, cut them loose. Find some friends with goals, dreams and aspirations. Get rid of as much negativity as you possibly can. You can't make others dream. Hold on to yours. You can inspire others. But they must be motivated for themselves.

Don't ever stop dreaming. You may have to make some adaptations, but always have a dream and a vision for yourself. There will be times when you are discouraged and may wonder if the press is worth it. When these times come, remember your dreams and goals. Encourage yourself by telling yourself of the world you dream of. Tell your dream!

Dreams
Hold fast to dreams for if dreams die,
Life is a broken-winged bird that cannot fly.
Hold fast to dreams for when dreams go,
Life is a barren field frozen with snow.
LANGSTON HUGHES

Questions

1. What is your dream?

2. Does your dream motivate you to work hard?

3. What do you visualize in your mind's eye about your future?

4. Do you wonder how you are going to make your dreams come true?

5. Do you realize that your worst handicap or negative situation can be used to make your dreams come true?

6. Many times kids who are focused (know where they are going) are criticized by their peers. Do you criticize the kids who know where they are going?

7. Are you awake to the potential and possibilities that life has for you or are you sleeping while life passes you by?

8. Are you taking advantage of all that is available to you to get ahead?

9. Do you ever reflect on what our ancestors did with the very little that they had?

10. How do you want future generations to remember you?

11. Have you written your short-term, mid-term and long-term goals yet?

Mother Wit

Yesterday is a canceled check; tomorrow is a promissory note; today is ready cash—use it. KAY LYONS

Don't be upset if your dreams don't come true. It could be the best thing that ever happened to you. SHARI BELAFONTE

When your dreams turn to dust, vacuum. DESMOND TUTU

Keep true to the dreams of your youth.
JOHANN VON SCHILLER

If one advances confidently in the directions of his dreams, and endeavors to live the life which he has imagined, he will meet with a success unexpected in common hours.
HENRY DAVID THOREAU

It's not what the dream is, it's what the dream does.
JOHN H. JOHNSON

All men and women of action are dreamers.
JAMES G. HUNEKER

It is difficult to say what is impossible, for the dream of yesterday is the hope of today and the reality of tomorrow.
ROBERT H. GODDARD

Some people dream of great accomplishments, while others stay awake and do them. CONSTANCE NEWMAN

Part III

Personal Management

Excellence is to do a common thing in an uncommon way.

Booker T. Washington

12
On Becoming a Woman of Excellence
(in speech, life, love, faith and purity)

"There are many fine women in the world, but you are the best of them all!" KING SOLOMON

When I entered first grade, I began receiving evaluations for my academic performance. They were called grades. A, B, C, D and F were the letters used to measure my level of performance, with A being the highest mark and F, the lowest. The teacher could add a plus or minus after each letter.

Pluses were intended to serve as encouragers, indicating that your work was above the actual letter grade you received, while minuses warned that you barely made it and that you were close to slipping. An A+ was the highest you could receive, and a D- was the lowest passing grade. My goal was to receive more A+'s and A's than anything else. An A+ was considered superior work and an A was regarded as excellent work. I didn't want less than an excellent evaluation.

I don't know exactly when it happened, but somewhere

along the line the grading system changed. When my children entered elementary school, the grading system consisted of E's for excellent, S's for satisfactory and NI's for needs improvement. The new system was designed partly to minimize the anxiety that was associated with letter grades. The teacher had the liberty to add a plus or minus after each letter with the new system if she felt the performance was above or below the three designations.

Under this system the goal was to receive more E's than anything else. Depending on your age, you may have experienced both systems. In either case, what were your goals? Are you pleased with your achievements so far? What are your goals for the future? My academic goals have been consistent with my life goals. I want to do the very best that I possibly can. I have appreciated those teachers and coaches who appealed to my potential, who would not accept less than my best. My mother, my first teacher, did not require that my siblings and I make straight A's in school. Some did some of the time and some did not. She did require that we put forth our best effort. I can still hear her asking, "Did you do your best? If you did your best, that's all that is required." These words served as both a challenge and encouragement.

I am grateful that I was not asked or expected to do that which is impossible. My best effort is possible, and I can successfully do that. Your best effort is also possible and you can enjoy success also. Nothing is better than your best effort. Your best effort may not result in straight A's, but you will have the assurance that you gave it your best shot. Not all of my evaluations have been the highest marks. I ran into some tough courses in college, namely chemistry and advanced music theory. I received C's in both classes. Both C's were like A's to me though, because I had worked very hard. I had given my best effort. I had nothing to be ashamed of. I refer to both C's as my Courage and Character evaluations. Courage, because I don't know another music major who took chemistry as their lab science; and Character, because I entered college barely knowing how to read music, but did what I had to do to not be behind my classmates. I earned the respect of both of my professors—one who humorously credits himself for my success in music because of the 'C' I received in his chemistry class, and the other who gave me my first professional performance opportunity. Both referred to me as an excellent student—not because I earned A's, but because of my effort.

You may never be listed on the honor roll for academic achievement, but you can put forth an excellent effort and receive excellent commendations. You may be thinking nobody is perfect. And this is true. But this truth is not an acceptable excuse for not doing your best. There is no excuse for not being excellent. Dr. William H. Cosby (a.k.a. Bill Cosby) gave his children names that begin with the letter E to encourage them to strive to be excellent. Your name may not begin with the letter E, but you can make excellence your aim also.

In my work as a musician, I have learned that a performance is never perfect, but it can always be excellent. An excellent effort will get excellent results. I have had the opportunity to perform many times by word of mouth—one conductor told another conductor about me and I was hired based on my reputation to deliver consistent quality performances. They felt comfortable hiring me because someone who was familiar with my work had highly recommended me. The best advertisement sometimes is word of mouth. (What is the word out about you?)

There are other musicians whose work I support because of their reputation. They have established themselves by their excellent work. I don't even need to hear their music before I buy it. I know that it will be excellent. You understand excellence. You demand it as a consumer. You have your favorite entertainers, designers, etc. They have won your allegiance through their consistent performance. Everyone appreciates excellence.

Excellence is attainable. It is a level of performance than can be achieved and maintained. Make it your life's goal—to be excellent in all of your endeavors. Your life and your work should be characterized by high quality and high standards. Consistent high-quality work will be rewarded.

You learn how to be excellent by observing and learning from those who are excellent. Do you remember back in Chapter One where I shared that there have been women, other than my mother, from whom I have learned and for whom I have great respect? I have been saving them until we got to this chapter, *On Becoming A Woman Of Excellence.* Each of these women possesses a prominent feature that is found in the portrait of a woman of excellence. I hope you enjoy meeting them.

Four women whom I love, from whom I have learned and for whom I have great respect are Mother Leola Copeland, Mrs. Barbara Tatum, Mrs. Valerian Summerville and Evangelist Ethel Caffie-Austin. While they share many of the same attributes, each lady represents a specific measure of excellence for me.

Mrs. Valerian Summerville, a.k.a. Punkin' and Lady, (and also my children's Godmother) represents a woman worthy of honor. Her generous spirit and purity of purpose has served as a source of strength for me for nearly twenty years. I celebrate my sister-friend Valerian. Strength and honor are her clothing and she shall rejoice in time to come.

Mrs. Barbara Tatum, a.k.a. the First Lady and Director of Christian Education at my church (Canaan Missionary Baptist Church of Urbana, Illinois) portrays a woman of dignity. She is a gifted teacher and I am honored to be numbered among her many students. Her attention to detail in every area (as a woman, wife, mother, grandmother, teacher and professional) has been most instructive to me. Sister Tatum is worthy of

112

great respect and I am pleased with this opportunity to thank her in print for all she means to me. Give her the fruit of her hands and let her own works praise her in the gates.

Mother Leola Copeland, a pastor's wife, mother of two, grandmother to three and Godmother to many, is the embodiment of confidence. In her quiet, yet confident manner, her influence is both a fact and a feeling. I treasure her words of wisdom and encouragement. Mother Copeland opens her mouth with wisdom and on her tongue is the law of kindness.

Evangelist Ethel Caffie-Austin. Where do I begin? She is a woman of virtue for whom I have the highest respect and affection. She is my role model, spiritual mother, mentor, friend, sister and confidante. I have known her for as long as I've known myself. (We grew up in the same hometown.) I am the beneficiary of her great teaching and counsel. She has influenced every part of my life, literally pouring her life into mine and charging me to bloom wherever I was planted. Sister Austin is the older sister in whom I confided, the good friend who encouraged me when I felt rejected and the one who comforted me when my mother died. I am pleased to be included in the great harvest that her life has produced. Many daughters have done well, but you, EJ, excel them all.

You know women from whom you have learned too. Tell them that you appreciate them. Show them your gratitude by becoming a woman of excellence from whom others learn.

Questions

1. What is your attitude regarding excellence?

2. Do you feel that adults are pushy to expect excellence from you?

3. What is your attitude about evaluations (grades)?

4. Do you have anxiety associated with your report card?

5. Do you understand the grading system used in your school? For example, how many points are required for an A, B, C, D, etc.?

6. What are your academic goals for next semester?

7. The author stated that her academic goals have been consistent with her life goals. There are many young people who have high life goals but accept low academic goals. Are you one of those young people?

8. Do you feel that it is uncool to make good grades or to have an international personality?

9. Who appeals to your potential and expects the best from you?

10. Tell the truth! Do you do your very best in school?

11. Are you happy about the word that is out about your performance in school and other areas of life?

12. How does the author say you learn to be excellent?

Mother Wit

Listen carefully to what the country people call mother wit. In those homely sayings are couched the collective wisdom of generations. MAYA ANGELOU

Of all the qualities necessary for success, none comes before character. ERNESTA PROCOPE

Excellence is to do a common thing in an uncommon way. BOOKER T. WASHINGTON

The will to win, the desire to succeed, the urge to reach your full potential. . . these are the keys that will unlock the door to personal excellence. EDDIE ROBINSON

We must use time as a tool; not as a couch. JOHN F. KENNEDY

Character is like a tree and reputation is like its shadow. The shadow is what we think of it; the tree is the real thing. ABRAHAM LINCOLN

If a man is called to be a streetsweeper, he should sweep streets even as Michelangelo painted, or as Beethoven composed music, or as Shakespeare wrote poetry. He should sweep streets so well that all the host of heaven and earth will pause to say, here lived a great streetsweeper who did his job well. MARTIN LUTHER KING, JR.

The greatest pleasure in life is being pleased with your own efforts. BLAIR UNDERWOOD

Violence of language leads to violence of action. Angry men seldom fight if their tongues do not lead the fray.

Charles V. Roman

13
Shooting from the Lip
(running off at the mouth)

To everything there is a season and a time to every purpose under the heavens writes King Solomon in Ecclesiastes 3. *A time to be born, and a time to die; a time to plant, and a time to pluck up that which is planted,* and so forth. There is a season and a time for everything we do while we are on planet earth. There is even a time to shoot from the lip (run off at the mouth) and a time to shut up (be quiet). Verse 7 states: *a time to keep silence, and a time to speak.*

Contrary to public opinion where you are encouraged to say what's on your mind all the time; and popular practice, where shooting from the lip and running off at the mouth among family, friends and foes is the thing to do, there is a time when silence is golden. There is a time when it is more profitable to hold your peace (be quiet) than to speak your mind (tell all that you're thinking). It's important to know what time it is.

My question for you is, "Can you tell time?" "Do you know what time it is, as it relates to when to keep silence and when to speak?" When my daughter Ashley was around 8 or 9, I taught her how to tell the time of day using an analog clock (one with numbers on the face). I had learned from previous experience that kids who have digital watches don't necessarily know how to tell time. They don't completely understand the relationship between the hours and minutes. They are able to read the numbers but do not comprehend what the numbers mean. There is more to understand regarding what time it is than just being able to read the numbers. There is more about knowing when to speak than just having an opinion. You need wisdom and discernment concerning when to speak and when not to speak.

About the same time that I was teaching Ashley how to tell time, I also talked to her about the time to keep silence and the time to speak. Being naturally inquisitive, curious and very well-spoken, she had a tendency to disclose (tell, reveal) whatever was on her mind. She frequently had a contribution to make to a conversation whether she was asked or not. While I didn't want to stifle or stunt her expressiveness, I knew that she needed to learn some restraint (control) in the area of talking. It is important for everyone to know when talking is appropriate and when it is not. Some things don't need to be commented on and some things just don't need to be said. I have known girls who talk just to hear themselves talk.

You hear them before you see them. You probably know some girls like this. There are girls who are quite beautiful until they open their mouths. Once you hear them speak, their beauty fades quickly. I don't want you to be one of them.

Have you ever said or thought, "I wish I hadn't said that?" or "I wish I could take that back," or "I didn't mean to say that." We've all felt that way. Our mouths are so eager to do damaging deeds. They can be so quickly engaged in action. While our words are still in our mouth, we are in control of them. But once our words leave our mouths, hit the wind and are carried away, the interpretation and impact of what we've said is up for grabs. No one has the luxury of saying anything and everything. Remember: *when you talk long, you increase*

118

your chance of talking wrong.

Before you run off at the mouth, take a quick survey. Ask yourself the following questions:

1. Are my comments good, bad or indifferent?
2. Does what I'm thinking need to be said? Does it add anything to the conversation?
3. Are my words compliments, complaints or criticism?
4. Will my words help someone stand tall or shrink on the inside?

Below are some suggested times when you should keep silence and when you should speak:

The Time To Speak

1. To speak the truth.
2. To disperse knowledge and wisdom.
3. To support others.
4. To judge righteously.

The Time To Keep Silence

1. When your words would damage others.
2. To brag about yourself.
3. When you don't know what you're talking about.
4. When you haven't heard the whole matter.
5. When your words are evil and false.

Questions

1. Are you good at determining when it is the right time to talk?

2. How do you rate yourself: an aggressive talker or a passive talker?

3. Is there substance (wisdom) in your talk or is it just about a lot of nothing?

4. What type of vocabulary do you have? Impressive for your age__ Average__ Needs help__

5. Do you know when to be quiet, weigh your words and speak only when appropriate?

6. When you are having a conversation, is it always time to speak when a good thought comes to your mind?

7. Do you ever use your mouth to talk about others in an immature and irresponsible way?

8. Have you wondered if there is a connection between how much a person talks and how insecure they feel?

9. How long has it been since you wanted to take back some words that you said?

10. Will your words help someone stand tall or shrink on the inside?

Mother Wit

Gossip is the opiate of the oppressed. ERICA JONG

Try to make the world laugh—it already has enough to cry about. RICHARD PRYOR

Some things are better left not said. BERNARD SHAW

The older he grew, the less he said, and the more he spoke. BENJAMIN E. MAYS

What you don't see with your eyes, don't invent with your tongue. JEWISH PROVERB

I have never been hurt by anything I didn't say. CALVIN COOLIDGE

When you shoot the arrow of truth, dip the point in honey. ANONYMOUS

Words are the most powerful drug used by mankind. RUDYARD KIPLING

Kind words can be short and easy to speak, but their echoes are truly endless. MOTHER TERESA

Language most shows a man or woman; speak, that I may see thee. BEN JOHNSON

Words should be weighed not counted. YIDDISH PROVERB

*All men that are ruined are ruined on
the side of their natural propensities.*
Edmund Burke

14
Addictions and Controllers
(contemporary slave masters)

One of the highlights of summer vacation when I was a child was the Carnival coming to town. It was our modest equivalent to the theme park of today—a humble form of entertainment. There were no fast roller coasters or rides that dropped you 75 feet in a matter of seconds. Probably the most aggressive ride was the Scrambler, and then there were the Ferris Wheel, Carousel and kiddie rides. There were booths for games of chance and vendors selling popcorn, cotton candy, hot dogs and candied apples. Bright lights lit up the night along with the sounds of kids screaming and laughing. I remember entering and immediately facing the dilemma of over-stimulation. What to do first? Eat? Play a game? Ride a ride? Decisions, decisions, decisions.

The Carnival was a welcomed sight to all of us children. But not to some parents, including my mother. She realized that the carnival was designed to manipulate and control us. The ultimate goal of the carnival was to get all of our spending change. The monotonous music playing, along with vendors yelling out for us to try our luck at their games could have an intoxicating effect upon us. My mother was aware of the lulling effect of being in a carnival environment. She knew that we could be easily influenced and enticed. By giving us only a little money, she provided a safeguard in case the lights and excitement dulled our senses.

Safeguards are important. To win in life you must have an effective defense. You need to set limits—decide how far you are going to go before you get there. Make a conscious decision before you are confronted. Particular temptations are associated with certain environments. One safeguard against having to deal with these temptations is to make sure you do not find yourself in these environments. It is very hard to win on foreign turf, where everything is unfamiliar and you don't understand the rules. Every team loves to have the home court advantage. Be aware of the lure and appeal of the strange.

The main reason why the Carnival was so appealing was its strangeness. It provided an escape from boredom, an interruption in the routine, and an altered state of consciousness (amusement). There were no worries at the carnival, no feelings of insecurity or of being unloved. It was another world—reality was placed on hold for a brief time.

Human nature has not changed much since my days as a child. There is still something exciting and exhilarating about taking risks, escaping reality and living on the edge. The testimonies of those who use addictive substances or engage in addictive activities, such as drugs, alcohol, tobacco, gambling, shopping, sex and so on, all have a similar ring to them—people are looking for a good time, wanting a temporary escape from the pressures of life, seeking a way of coping, and so on. Everyone thinks that they can handle what they become involved in. They believe that they can separate the pleasure of the moment from the penalty and pain that comes later. Nowhere is the flip side of the coin shown. Only the enjoyment is advertised.

The consequences for yielding to temptation never seem to

be as severe as they eventually become. The attempt to escape from bad circumstances often leads to worse ones; and the attempt to experience the ultimate high may lead to a pitiful and desperate low. Compulsive behavior is not on a person's itinerary, but is often their destination. Addiction is no joke! Ask anyone trying to recover. Among the many things that a grateful recovering addict will share are these two phrases *"Hindsight is 20/20"* and *"If I knew then, what I know now, I would have done things differently."* These are words uttered from the voice of experience. Both phrases suggest regret about a bad decision or poor choice.

Hindsight and 20/20 refer to vision. Hindsight is the ability to look back and see what should have been done a long time ago. Twenty-twenty is the ability to see clearly at twenty feet what the normal eye sees at that distance. Have you ever said, "I see it now," when you wished that you had done something differently? It is your hindsight that recognizes that there was possibly a better way. After the fact things become very clear. Life is filled with opportunities to develop perfect hindsight. Hindsight is useful when it produces some insight (understanding).

Insight is the ability to know, understand and apply wisdom while making decisions in life. We are experiencing insight when we say, "I see what you mean." "We see" actually means, "we understand." To "see what is meant" is "to know or understand what is meant." As you navigate through life you will have many opportunities to apply insight. Besides hindsight and insight, you also need foresight, which is the ability to know or see beforehand. This talk about addictions and controllers, those contemp-orary slavemasters, is intended to give you some insight and encourage you to use some foresight.

Addictions will kill you. In one way or another, addictions are designed to take you out. They will kill your creativity, your intellect, credibility, character and possibly take your life. If you are curious about the effect of drugs, alcohol, cigarettes and other substances, don't try them out. Instead, go and find people who work with addicts and ask them. Benefit from another's knowledge and information. Experience is a good teacher, but it is not the only teacher. You do not need to experience everything first-hand to know about it. You can never be too careful. Always be cautious if there is any danger involved, or if the consequences are severe. There are some mistakes in life that you can't take back. See the result of an activity by observing someone else's life before you subject yourself to the same consequences.

I formed my convictions regarding addictive substances and activities by observing the conse-quences in others' lives. I decided early that I would not be brought under the power of any. There were temptations and many opportunities to smoke, drink and run around when I was a teenager. My mother told me the negative consequences of such behavior, but what was most instructive were the visuals I witnessed. To this day, when I read the word addict, I have a vivid picture in my mind. I see a place and some people. Let me see if I can paint the picture.

Almost every neighborhood has at least one. It is practically an institution in the Black community. It's a place where a lot of intellectual exchange takes place—where business is transacted. And for the most part, it's a place to shoot the breeze. In some neighborhoods, it's a barbershop. In my hometown, it was the corner.

When I was coming up there was always a group of men who held up the corner at South Virginia Avenue and Main Street. From sunup to sundown, winter, spring, summer and fall, you could find someone standing there. Drinking wine. Smoking cigarettes. Watching women. Checking out cars. It was a meeting place where business was conducted and where there was talk about ships coming in. They didn't really bother anybody, nor were they bothered. But even as a child it was a sad sight to see.

Various circumstances contributed to the formation of the corner crowd—unemployment, substance abuse, idleness, lack of a work ethic and lack of job skills, to name a few. When I was a kid, men old enough to be my father held up the corner. By the time I graduated high school, men in their twenties were there and when I go home now for visits, teenagers are at the post. The corner represents a slow death. I watched people deteriorate until finally you didn't see them out there anymore. As one would die, someone else would take his place.

The corner represented a slow death, much like addiction. Decide early not to be brought under the power of any!

Questions

1.What forms of entertainment manipulate and control the young people of today?

2. Have you ever gotten involved with something you thought that you could handle but ended up being handled by it?

3. Do you know of anyone who started out with addiction as a destination?

4. Do you know of a drug addict who hit bottom?

5. How do you feel about advertisements for alcohol, beer and cigarettes?

6. Are you the type who has to learn everything for herself?

7. When the subject of drugs is mentioned, what vivid picture comes your mind?

8. Do you believe there can be unlimited pleasure without any pain?

9. Is anything controlling you right now?

10.Do you feel that getting high changes anything?

11.Where is the place in your community where the brothers hang out?

Mother Wit

The freedom of slaves is measured by the length of their chains.
JOSEPHÍNE BAKER

All men that are ruined are ruined on the side of their natural propensities. EDMUND BURKE

Wine is a mocker, strong drink is raging: and whosoever is deceived thereby is not wise. KING SOLOMON

Whose heart is filled with anguish and sorrow? Who is always fighting and quarreling? Who is the man with bloodshot eyes and many wounds? It is the one who spends long hours in the taverns, trying out new mixtures. KING SOLOMON

Cocaine told me she loved me, but never said she'd lead me to the county jail. TODD BRIDGES

O God, that men [and women] should put an enemy in their mouths to steal away their brains! That we should, with joy, pleasance, revel, and applause, transform ourselves into beasts! WILLIAM SHAKESPEARE

What is dangerous about the tranquilizers is that whatever peace of mind they bring is packaged peace of mind. Where you buy a pill and buy peace with it, you get conditioned to cheap solutions instead of deep ones. MAX LERNER

Nothing but ruin stares a nation in the face that is a prey to the drink habit. MOHANDAS GANDHI

No man [or woman] is above the law and no man is below it: nor do we ask any man's permission when we ask him to obey it.

Theodore Roosevelt

15
The Principle of Authority and Submission
(r.e.s.p.e.c.t.)

When I took my oldest daughter Kirstie to campus for college orientation, she made only one request before leaving home—*Mother, please don't make me carry one of those orange bags. That is the badge of being a freshman. I don't want everyone to know that I'm an incoming freshman, because freshman get no respect.* Her request seemed reasonable. I remembered my college days, so I complied. We did not carry an orange bag at her freshman orientation.

Every place has a hierarchy or pecking order. In schools among students, the hierarchy is determined by grade level. The higher the grade level the more respect you are given. In other words, if you are an upperclassman, you do the pecking; and if you are an underclassman, you receive the pecking. This practice assumes that with age comes experience; and with experience comes wisdom; and with wisdom comes respect. The older you are, the more experience you have. And the more experience you have, the more wisdom you should have. So age, experience, and wisdom are among the accepted conditions for receiving respect. As a college freshman, Kirstie will more than likely be among the youngest, the least experienced, and the most unfamiliar with the routine on campus—conditions for receiving little, if any respect. She will have to earn respect in ways other than age advantage, namely through her discipline and demeanor.

Everyone wants respect. You can do without a lot of things, but it's hard to do without respect. Disrespect causes many altercations (fights) among people. *(Give me my props* [respect]—"don't diss me" is a common cry). Respect is something that we give to others, but it is also something that we must earn from others. You cannot demand that someone respect you. You must live a life that is worthy of respect. The amount of respect you receive is up to you. Here are some conditions that must be met in order for you to be respected!

1. You earn the respect of others by first respecting yourself. It is not something that is freely given. You work for it. You show others that you respect yourself in many identifiable ways. Let's consider three—your language, your attitude and your behavior.

Does your vocabulary sound like you picked it out of a trash can—loud, lewd and full of profanity? Does your behavior demonstrate that you consider yourself valuable or cheap? Are you laid up on boys out in public in an inappropriate way? And thirdly, does your attitude serve you well by showing that you are positive and pleasant, or are you described as difficult, at best? Before you get upset, and cry that you've been dissed, answer the following question, do you respect yourself?

No one can make you feel disrespected without your participation. Show respect for yourself by guarding your speech, behavior and attitude. Respect yourself and you will be considered worthy of someone else's respect.

2. Another way to receive respect is to give respect. When you respect others, you place yourself in a position to receive respect. Give and it shall be given to you, pressed down, shaken together and running over. Give respect to others and remember that you reap what you sow. If you are giving respect to others you will receive respect eventually. It may not come from those you give it to, but you will see a return on your investment.

Respect for elders was part of a code of behavior when I was growing up. It didn't matter who they were, *respect your elders* was a universal concept. If they were a generation or more older than you, they were worthy of your respect. Gray hair was a coveted symbol of wisdom. Old age was cause for admiration and respect. Even if you didn't want to hear what an elderly person said, you were expected to stand there, listen and be polite. And if an older person said anything to us that we did not like, we would be in double trouble if we said anything back. We were taught to respect the person's age. There was a time when an older person could correct someone younger without any fear of being disrespected. Age gave them license to tell you something that they thought was for your good.

I remember my father-in-law saying whatever he wanted to say, whenever he felt like it, and to whomever he wanted to. My husband and his siblings would say, *Pops, why do you have to say that?* They would be more than a little embarrassed about his conversation or choice of words at times. Now, he was not offensive. Maybe a bit forward, but never offensive. Remembering my upbringing I would quickly come to his defense and say, *If you live to be 80, then you can say whatever you want to say too.*

There are many areas where one should be given respect. Age is one area, and authority is another. If you find it difficult to respect the person, you should respect the position they hold.

Don't worry about the person, just don't be found guilty of being out of line. I grew up with clear, steadfast rules about being properly aligned.

Trouble at school constituted double jeopardy. If we disrespected authority, we placed ourselves in a no-win situation. The teacher could have been dead wrong. But we weren't suppose to take the matter into our hands. I remember only one time trying to defend myself at school. I thought that I would be rewarded for setting the record straight. Instead, I was scolded for being disrespectful. I hadn't figured in that falling out with one authority figure (the teacher) placed me in greater jeopardy at home (with my mother). When I got home and related the incident to my mother, her response was chilling. *So, you think you're grown, huh? You didn't need for me to handle the situation. You think you're grown?* She really was saying *since* you think you're grown. It felt terrible to hear those words. They cut deeply. I learned that adults take care of adult business and children take care of children business. I was totally out of order trying to deal with the adult authority. There was no excuse good enough for not respecting an adult, in other words, what I had done was inexcusable.

I attribute my wonderful relationship with my mother to the fact that I understood the relationship. My mother was the authority, period! I never forgot, not for one minute, that she was in charge. Even as a teenager and young adult, it never crossed my mind to consider myself her equal. We laughed together, played games, talked and generally cut up, but I was never on her level. There could only be one woman in our house at a time, and she made it clear to all of us that she was that woman. You did what she said or the same door that brought you in could take you out. She would add, "And don't let the door catch you as you leave." I learned early to shut up, and wait my turn.

I will always be my mother's daughter. I will not always be

a child, but I will always be her daughter. And respecting our relationship of mother to daughter, we are properly aligned. I respected her because I loved her. I respected her because of her age, and also because I feared her.

I had a very healthy fear of my mother. Actually, it was a healthy respect and reverence for her. She required that we respect her and she lived a life before us that was worthy of respect. My mother did not play. No talking back. Now, I could express my opinion, but I had better use a respectful tone of voice. She taught me that it is not only what you have to say that's important, but also how you say it. No sassing, as she would say. She didn't care how old you were. When you were in her house, she was in charge. I was raised to be self-reliant, independent and ambitious, but there was never a question as to who was in charge in my home when I was growing up. My mother was the authority figure. She taught me the principle of authority and submission and that teaching has served me well.

There are two things I want for you to remember regarding authority and submission.

1. Respect those who are older than you.
2. Respect those who are placed over than you.

Questions

1. Do you agree that age, experience and wisdom are conditions for receiving respect?

2. What are some ways, besides age, to earn respect?

3. Do you respect yourself?

4. In what ways do you show respect to others?

5. What authority figure do you have the biggest problem with?

6. If you are mistreated by an authority figure, how do you respond?

7. What concrete steps are you taking to help you deal wisely with the authority in your life?

8. Do you ever feel rebellious for no apparent reason?

9. Do you listen to music or rap that encourages rebellion?

10. Are you planting seeds of respect, knowing that in time you will reap respect?

Mother Wit

Rules are for the obedience of fools and the guidance of wise men. DAVID OGILVY

For the policeman does not frighten people who are doing right; but those doing evil will always fear him. PAUL OF TARSUS

Only a fool despises his father's advice; a wise son considers each suggestion. KING SOLOMON

The highest duty is to respect authority. LEO XIII

Most powerful is he who has himself in his own power. SENECA

No man [or woman] is above the law and no man is below it: nor do we ask any man's permission when we ask him to obey it. THEODORE ROOSEVELT

You can stand tall without standing on someone. You can be a victor without having victims. HARRIET WOODS

Agree with thine adversary quickly, whiles thou art in the way with him; lest at any time the adversary deliver thee to the judge, and the judge deliver thee to the officer, and thou be cast into prison. JESUS CHRIST

Strive to make something of yourself;
then strive to make the most
of yourself.
Alexander Crummell

16
How to Learn When You Feel Your Teacher Doesn't Like You
(staying on task)

Ninth grade algebra was challenging for me. It wasn't because I didn't understand the subject matter. I really enjoyed math, and did well academically, but I didn't enjoy the environment. I felt that my teacher did not like me. It wasn't all my imagination either. She gave me more than a few reasons to feel this way. If I raised my hand to ask a question, she tried to ignore me. If she did acknowledge me, she used a nasty tone of voice to answer the question. This woman had a serious attitude. I wanted to go off on her more times than I care to mention. But because of my home training, that was not a viable option. The only way I could break even was to perform well academically.

My experience in a class with a teacher who didn't like me and didn't try to hide it really impacted me. The thing that was more hurtful than her tone of voice or sarcasm was the grades she gave me for citizenship and attitude. She couldn't affect my performance grade, but she would give me less than desirable attitude grades. From this, I knew that it was something personal and often wondered what I had done to make her not like me.

For many years I had problems with women with red hair and freckles and never really understood why. I had a level of distrust towards them. I would find myself being gracious with them but never getting too close. My breakthrough came one summer when I worked in an office with a young lady with red hair and freckles. I couldn't understand how I could get along with her or enjoy being in her company. Then one day I made the connection. I thought I couldn't get along with freckled redheads because my ninth grade algebra teacher was a freckled redhead and I couldn't get along with her. I remember telling my coworker about my experience with redheads and thanking her for helping me to heal from my scars.

What do you do when you feel that people in authority over you, such as teachers, coaches and sponsors, don't like you? Here are some things to help you do what you have to do, even when you don't want to.

1. Evaluate yourself. Have you had a bad attitude, rolled your eyes at this person or done something that would make them dislike you? Have you been confrontational or disrespectful or anything of that nature? If you have not done anything, then you must decide to go on and get your job done. Don't worry about being popular with this person, just determine to fulfill your responsibilities. If you have offended the person, do the right thing—apologize and work out a way to maintain a cordial relationship.

2. Do your job. To succeed in life, you must learn to fulfill your responsibilities regardless of how others treat you. This is what I had to do. I had to get the job done and deal with my grades. The attitude grade was her opinion over mine because she was the teacher. There was nothing I could do about that, but the academic performance grade was up to me. I saved my papers in case I needed documentation to support what I felt was fair. I encourage you to do the same.

3. Realize that you do not have to be liked to learn. One of the problems of being young is that you want everybody to like you. As you get older you will realize that there will be times when you must go to school or work with people who do not like you.

4. Find out if this person has problems with other people also. In the case of my teacher, she was having her own personal problems (going through a nasty divorce) and had selected several of us in her class to take her frustrations out on. This is unfair but it happens everyday. It is called misdirected anger.

5. Make the decision to do what you have to do. I was there to get an education, not to win a popularity contest. If I had stood up in her face and challenged her word for word I would have been expelled from school. I had to hold my tongue. It was not worth getting kicked out of school. Success in life comes as a result of making the right decisions. Pressing on in the face of opposition is the key to having a successful life. You must decide to learn from experiences such as this and use them to gain strength for future challenges that are sure to come.

6. Remember that there are certain battles that you are not supposed to fight. Young people are not supposed to fight adult battles. When you have a problem with an adult, you are not qualified to challenge that adult. You must take your problem to another adult who will serve as your advocate and properly handle the situation. This person could be a parent, aunt, uncle, grandfather, grandmother or school counselor.

141

It is important to remember that a problem with a teacher or an authority figure should never disqualify all teachers or authority figures. Give each individual the benefit of doubt. Let them show themselves. Don't prejudge. It is human to have differences with people occasionally, and it is healthy to get healed from them and move on.

Questions

1. Have you ever had a teacher that did not like you? What concrete reasons have led you to this conclusion?

2. How has your home training prepared you to deal with the negative attitudes of others?

3. Do you protect yourself in class or on the job by doing what is right and having a professional attitude?

4. Do you realize that people can dislike you for no apparent reason? Do you question yourself when you dislike someone for no apparent reason?

5. Do you have problems with a particular type of person as a result of trouble that happened in the past?

6. Are you one of those types who is never wrong?

7. Are you stuck on the fact that "life is unfair"?

8. Do you choose your battles wisely?

9. Do you treat others as individuals?

10. Finally, are you considering becoming a teacher?

Mother Wit

If there is no struggle, there is no progress.
FREDERICK DOUGLASS

Never cut what you can untie. JOSEPH JOUBERS

We owe almost all our knowledge not to those who have agreed, but to those who have differed. CHARLES CALEB COLTON

Chance makes our parents, but choice makes our friends. JACQUES DELILLE

Perhaps the most valuable result of all education is the ability to make yourself do the thing you have to do, when it ought to be done, whether you like it or not. WALTER BAGEHOT

A teacher is the child's third parent. HYMAN MAXWELL BERTON

Strive to make something of yourself; then strive to make the most of yourself. ALEXANDER CRUMMELL

A teacher affects eternity; he/she can never tell where their influence stops. HENRY ADAMS

Don't measure yourself by what you have accomplished, but by what you should have accomplished with your ability. BEN CHAVIS

Success is difficult; it's gut-wrenching and pain-inducing. PARREN MITCHELL

17
I Was Treated Unfairly Today
(∂oing right when you've been ∂one wrong)

O n the way home one day from picking up my daughter Ashley, I decided to make a quick stop at the drugstore. The plan was to run in, get what I needed, and run out. The long line at the check-out counter was not exactly in the plan, so when I heard a voice saying no waitin' (waiting) in camera, we made our way there. There was no waiting at the counter in camera, but we did experience some hatin' (hating). What should have been a simple transaction turned into an object lesson.

We were the first to arrive at the camera department and proceeded to place our items on the counter. The cashier rang up the items. So far, so good. I handed her my credit card. She swiped the card. Still, so far, so good. What happened next was not good. After she saw that the transaction had been approved, she threw my card on the counter. I was confronted with a moment of decision. I stood there for a few moments, which felt like several minutes, trying to decide which impulse to choose.

My first impulse was to go totally off and ask her what her

problem was. This would have made me feel good at first, but I would have caused a big scene and embarrassed Ashley and myself. So, I waited for another impulse. My second impulse was to tell her that I didn't want the stuff, to credit my account, that my money was green and that I could shop somewhere else. This would have caused a smaller scene, but would have taken up the time I was trying to save. I would have had to go to another store to get the items. So, I waited a little longer. Finally, a third impulse arrived. I chose to act upon my third impulse.

I picked up my card, looked at the cashier and said, "Did I throw my card on the counter?" Without waiting for her to respond, I continued, "No, I handed my card to you. And because I handed my card to you, I expect you to hand my card back to me." I then handed my card back to her, and in turn, she handed it back to me. She then proceeded to tell me that she didn't mean to offend me. I told her that I had been offended and that it was important to me that I receive the same courtesy that I give. I left the store feeling good because I had handled the situation properly and had not been handled by the situation. This incident also provided a perfect object lesson for my daughter on how to do right when you've been done wrong.

My daughter's presence played a major role in the steps I followed to handle this offense. I was very upset. No, actually I was hot. I could feel my body heat. As I replayed the events of the situation back to the lady who had offended me, I had time to cool down. The time I took to recount the incident actually helped me to maintain a sense of control. I told the story as I understood it, without putting any emotion into it or making it a personal attack. I just told what I thought had happened, which included what she had done and what I had done, what I wanted her to do and why I wanted her to do it. When you find yourself in a potentially volatile situation, try to be as objective as possible. Use the following questions to help you:

1. What is the problem?
2. What part did I play in creating the problem?
3. What part did the other person play in creating the problem?
4. What am I willing to do to help solve the problem?
5. What do I want the other person to do to help solve the problem?

It will be easier to do right when you've been done wrong if you realize a few things.

1. You reap what you sow.

You can let a lot slide. It will be taken care of sooner or later. Anyone who does you wrong will eventually get what's coming to them. It will save you a lot of trouble if you just let circumstances take care of themselves.

2. With people, there is usually more than meets the eye.

You need the ability to discern and see what is really going on. The lady at the register was having her own problems. She was frustrated, trapped in her position and very unhappy about it. Now, that is no excuse for poor service. But I have to be fair and realize that some people are very unhappy with the life they are living, whether as a result of their own choosing or not. The laughter and fun I was having with my daughter may have been too much for her that day. She needed some ministering to, not meanness.

3. You have control over your own feelings.

No one can make you mad. It is your own choice whether or not to get mad. You don't have to go off at every infraction. You can maintain self-control. To react to every offense would be to allow someone to control you. I am not willing to allow people to overturn my cart. I will not give up my peace of mind, joyful spirit or positive attitude for anyone. My joy is my strength. My peace is my contentment. My positive attitude is my energy. There will be times when you are treated unfairly. You will be confronted with some choices on how to respond, just as I was. So many possibilities flashed before me. It took a lot of power not to sound off. Your ego will make some suggestions. Your emotions will also make some suggestions. The voice of reason will speak too, if you allow it. What will you do? What advice will you heed?

Questions

1. What did you do the last time you were treated unfairly?

2. When you are treated unfairly do you assess the situation before you respond? Are you able to stay objective?

3. What lessons have you learned from the negative things that happen to you?

4. Do you believe that you respond to people based on how you feel about yourself?

5. In your opinion, why can strong people ignore the insults of the weak?

6. Do you have the ability to discern what is going on behind the scenes when someone mistreats you?

7. What are some reasons you can do right when you've been done wrong?

Mother Wit

Hate is like acid. It can damage the vessel in which it is stored as well as destroy the object on which it is poured.
ANN LANDERS

We must define ourselves by the best that is in us, not the worst that has been done to us. EDWARD LEWIS

Don't hate, it's too big a burden to bear.
MARTIN LUTHER KING, SR

Don't quarrel with anyone. Be at peace with everyone, just as much as possible. PAUL OF TARSUS

All cruelty springs from weakness. SENECA

Half of the harm that is done in this world is due to people who want to feel important. They don't mean to do harm—but the harm does not interest them. T. S. ELIOT

Prejudice is feeling without reason. MAX GRALNICK

Rudeness is the weak man's imitation of strength.
ERIC HOFFER

If you have been a fool by being proud or plotting evil, don't brag about it—cover your mouth with your hand in shame.
KING SOLOMON

The best manner of avenging ourselves is by not resembling him who has injured us. JANE PORTER

150

18
Free at Last!
(delivered from the pain of the past)

"Floats like a butterfly
stings like a bee,
I told (whomever)
not to mess with me."
MUHAMMED ALI

This phrase is probably foreign to you, but when I was your age it was widely known and maybe as popular as *like Mike, I wanna be like Mike.* There has never been a figure in the world of boxing as widely heralded as the Greatest, the incomparable Muhammed Ali. As Iron Mike (Tyson) is to some, and The Real Deal (Evander Holyfield) is to others, Muhammed Ali (The Greatest) is to my generation. He was a national icon (symbol).

A large part of Ali's appeal was his verbal banter and calisthenics that led up to the actual match. He was handsome, he knew it and he made sure everyone else knew it too. He would often say how *pretty* he was. He was witty. He used many statements to describe his ability. And he made good on his word in the ring. It is said that his punches had a serious sting to them. If you are unfamiliar with the Champ, you owe it to yourself to go to the library or a video store and get a video of him when he was in his prime. His smack (boasting and bragging) and his shuffle (the Ali shuffle) are well worth your while.

Have you ever been stung by a bee? If you have, you know that it is a painful ordeal. It feels like your skin is being twisted in a grip. In the case of a worker honeybee sting, your skin *is* twisted to some extent. When a worker honeybee stings, her barbed, needle-sharp stinger firmly anchors itself in the flesh of its victim. In her attempt to withdraw the stinger and break free, she tears away part of her abdomen and dies shortly afterwards. The fact that she dies after the sting is very satisfying. It's also comforting to know that she can only sting once.

She has the power to hurt one time and one time only. This is good news! Relief and healing from the pain of the sting depends on locating the stinger and removing it. And the sooner the better. I don't know about you, but I have been stung before, both externally (physically, i.e. bee stings) and internally (emotionally, i.e. hurt feelings). In either case, the only way to get relief is to identify the source of the pain, locate the stinger and release its grip. Deliverance is a deliberate decision. You must decide to no longer be bound and held hostage by painful memories of past hurts.

In this instance, you must initiate your own freedom. And just like being stung by a worker honeybee, the actual things that have happened to you have lost the power to hurt you again. If painful memories from a hurt that happened long ago are not dealt with, they will continue to control you until your perspective and understanding of the past changes. It's possible to stay under the spell of false memories.

Let me encourage you to deal with the painful emotions and memories from your past. I know that it is not easy, but you owe it to yourself to break free. Your future depends on it. I understand that it may be difficult and that in some instances you may feel that you just "can't get over it." I'm not going to add insult to your injury by telling you to just *get over it*, but I am going to challenge you to *get beyond it*. Use the following steps to put your healing and recovery into motion:

Step 1. Release painful memories. Let go of fear, hurt, shame, disappointment and whatever other emotions are attached to the memory of a painful experience. Acknowledge that you have been hurt and that you have had a host of emotions about this, but decide that you will not hold on to painful memories.

Step 2. Correct your emotional responses to painful memories. If you have been hurt and you feel bitter, angry and resentful, you need to forgive the one who has wronged you. Forgiveness is for us. It frees us from emotional hurt and gives us emotional wholeness. Forgiveness goes deep to the level of the spirit so that we can be emotionally whole and healthy. You can't change what has happened to you, but you can choose your response to it. You can choose your attitude in any given circumstance.

Step 3. Get a new perspective on a painful memory. What was the motivation behind a past hurt? Was there anything happening in the life of the person who wronged you that contributed to the hurt you experienced?

Step 4. Be patient with yourself. Memories exist in layers. After you deal with the surface, move to another layer, and go forth. Healing from painful memories is a process. Remember you need to recognize the pain, identify what caused the pain, and release its grip in your life. This process begins with forgiving the person who has wronged you.

Pain has a purpose. We usually don't mind going through

something if we are better off when we come out of it, or we feel like it has been worth it. Much of what I've shared with you has been painful for me. But I don't mind sharing my pain if it is for your gain. I've learned to make my pain count. It yields a profit. I don't want to suffer for nothing. And you shouldn't either. Let me encourage you to move beyond the immobilizing effect of pent-up painful memories. Don't let the pain from past hurts paralyze your present and cripple your future. Instead, let the pain that seems to bind you, help remind you that it is powerless, and that the hurt is really behind you.

Questions

1. Have you ever been stung emotionally? Is the stinger still in your or have your removed it?

2. Review the four steps to begin your healing. Which of the four do you find most challenging?

3. Can you make a private list of the pain and hurt that you have experienced that no one knows about but you? Then you can decide which memory to deal with first.

4. What brings freedom and emotional wholeness?

5. Do you feel it is possible to choose your attitude in any circumstance?

6. Are you mature enough to give people some slack when they are temporarily stressed? Do you expect others to give you some slack when you are stressed?

7. If you could change one thing about your life, what would it be?

8. After reading this chapter, do you feel that you are better able to handle your pent-up painful memories? Be patient, it will take time.

Mother Wit

It's better to look where you are going than to see where you have been. FLORENCE GRIFFITH-JOYNER

This is a tough game. There are times when you've got to play hurt, when you've got to block out the pain.
SHAQUILLE O'NEAL

To accept one's past—one's history—is not the same thing as drowning in it; it is learning how to use it. An invented past can never be used; it cracks and crumbles under the pressures of life like clay in a season of drought. JAMES BALDWIN

We are all serving a life sentence in the dungeon of self.
CYRIL CONNOLLY

There is no way to know before experiencing.
ROBERT ANTHONY

Enough is enough! FANNIE LOU HAMER

Everything in the household runs smoothly when love oils the machinery. WILLIAM H. GRIER

Only our individual faith in freedom can keep us free.
DWIGHT D. EISENHOWER

The basic test of freedom is perhaps less in what we are free to do than in what we are free not to do. ERIC HOFFER

The events of childhood do not pass but repeat themselves like seasons of the year. ELEANOR FARJEON

156

Part IV

The Real Deal Regarding Relationships

If a man does not keep pace with his companions, perhaps it is because he hears a different drummer. Let him step to the music which he hears, however measured or far away.

Henry David Thoreau

19
You and Your Peers
(are you applying pressure or being pressed?)

Have you ever heard the phrase "birds of a feather flock together?" Its meaning is quite clear—people who have things in common, hang around together. Those who hang around together are called "peers." A peer group is sort of like a gang with the potential to be very powerful and productive. People who put their resources and energy toward a common goal can accomplish quite a bit. There are service organizations and clubs that do a lot of good in communities across the nation. The power of an idea or vision holds these groups together. What keeps you a part of your peer group?

Interaction over long periods of time will reveal the real elements that hold a group together. Be careful if your peer group revolves around one individual. There should be equality among the individuals on the horizontal relating field (group). You will be closer to some girls than others, but with every relationship there must be common courtesy and mutual respect. Also, beware of things that seem like strengths in others such as a strong personality, persuasive verbal skills, lack of self-restraint and disregard for others. What a person is really like and their real interests will eventually come out.

Every relationship has its moment of truth. Determine what the attraction is. Don't compromise your convictions in order to be included in a group. You need people who will support you and be kind and constructive in their criticism of you. You will have friends and you will have enemies. In order to have the right friends, you must be willing to have the right enemies. Be wise and do not confuse who should fall into which category.

Don't underestimate the power of your peer group. It is incredibly influential and has the power to compel you to think a certain way. Throughout the rest of your life, you will have to deal with peer pressure. How will you handle it? A young lady in our youth group gave the best response that I know. When she was asked: "How are you *handling* peer pressure?" She replied, "I am not *handling* peer pressure, I *am* peer pressure." She was saying that she set the standard. She established the reference point. I remember my husband saying to her, "You go, girl."

If I asked you the same question, what would you say? Are you applying positive peer pressure or are you being pressed? Think about whom you influence and who influences you as you read this chapter. The best way to deal with peer pressure is to be peer pressure. Operate in your peer group from a position of strength. Know who you are and what you believe. The best defense is a good offense. Horizontal relationships with family and friends are nice and necessary. They require a lot of energy and effort. Supportive, healthy relationships are worth all the effort and work you invest in them. Build strong, healthy friendships. The way to build healthy friendships is by being a good friend. Be the type of friend that you would like to have.

Here are some characteristics of a healthy friendship:

1. There is unconditional acceptance and appreciation.
2. There is genuine interest and concern.
3. There is sincere praise.
4. There is faithfulness, loyalty and availability.
5. There is sensitivity and support.
6. There is honesty (the truth spoken with love).

There are "friends" who pretend to be friends, but there is
a friend who sticks closer than a brother.
KING SOLOMON

All relationships exist because of the possibility of getting one's needs met. You may have the need to encourage someone, so you hang with a peer who needs encouragement. Or, you may be the one who needs some encouragement, so you have a peer who is an encourager. Relationships grow and intensify as long as needs are being met. What does your peer group do for you? Have you considered what your needs are? How deeply do you need to belong? And why do you need to belong?

Peers are those people in your life who are your age, give or take a couple of years; with whom you have things in common; and with whom you spend time. The intensity and intimacy of peer relationships vary, depending on what you have to give and what you need to receive. There are different levels of friendship.

The first level of friendship is the acquaintance level. Contact is infrequent but cordial and the conversation is very general. What is shared is considered public information.

The next level of friendship is the associate level, where the conversation is casual and the contact is based on common interests and activities. Conversation at the associate level of

161

friendship asks specific questions about opinions (What would you do?), goals (What are you planning?) and ideas (What do you think?).

The third level of friendship is the close friendship level. The fellowship is very frequent and revolves around mutual life goals. The conversation includes advice about everything.

The fourth level of friendship is the most intimate. Those peers that you see often, share with and generally kick it with, are considered your *girls*, or your *girlfriends*. As the levels become more intimate, the number of girls becomes smaller. You have a lot of acquaintances, many associates, some close friends and a few, and sometimes only one best girlfriend. Who are the girls in your life? Do you have peers who fall into each category? Acquaintance? Associate? Friend? Girlfriend?

What does each girl in your peer group bring to your life? What do you contribute to each girl's life? At each level, you are influenced and you have influence.

You have the right to choose who your best friends are. Just because someone considers you her best friend doesn't mean she is your best friend. Always be truthful. Honesty must be at the foundation of every relationship. Be careful not to allow anyone to manipulate you. A real friend wants the very best for you and does not prey on your fears, weaknesses and insecurities.

The opening phrase, *"birds of a feather flock together,"* warns you to guard your reputation. Don't be found guilty because of your association. People assume that those who hang together share similar beliefs and behavior. I heard this admonition when I tried to justify my choice of running partners that my mother didn't necessarily agree with. Who protects you from choosing less than desirable running partners? What do they say to you?

Having girlfriends is a lot of fun. And then sometimes girls can be messy. They do what they do with such intensity. They can be beautiful and they can be brutal. When they like you and are supportive, life is wonderful. But when they criticize and have attitudes against you, life can be miserable. We are social beings. Everyone wants to win friends and have some influence upon people. In addition to wanting to get ahead, we want to get along. And for girls, getting along is sometimes more difficult than getting ahead. Conflict within female relationships can be a huge hindrance and distraction to achievement. Conflict can also be the beginning of personal growth. Challenging situations are opportunities to learn what you are made of. There are some things that are best learned the hard way.

All relationships do not grow more intimately. At times, relationships among peers plummet downward. There are times of inevitable fall-out when a friendship disintegrates to barely being on speaking terms. There are many reasons for this including, but not limited to, the talking behind the back syndrome, the sounding off in front of others exercise, the he-said, she-said rhetoric, and the plain and simple growing apart reality. All relationships should not grow more intimately.

Unhealthy alliances should be corrected or cut off. This can be difficult. But it is vitally necessary. Here are two things to consider as you examine your relationships:

1. Who are the terrorists? Identify any misguided, self-appointed leaders who force their way and opinion over everyone else's. Ask yourself, Am I respected as an individual? Am I being terrorized or traumatized? Am I appreciated for who I am? Be an individual. Maintain your distinction. Decide you are content to be alone if necessary.

2. Who are the temptresses? Recognize any subtle ways that you are encouraged to act unacceptably. Beware of verbal and non-verbal innuendo regarding decisions and choices. Ask yourself, "What is the motivation behind the suggested behavior or belief? (Why does this person want me to do this or believe this?) Is my personal opinion seen as important or even regarded? Do I have to go along in order to be accepted?" Be an independent thinker.

Root out all terrorists and temptresses from among your relationships Every friendship will not be smooth sailing. Some friendships go through rocky stages, but eventually level out. Don't bail out too quickly, give the relationship some time. Don't allow occasional moodiness to mess up a rewarding relationship. But if after you've waited to see if things will work out and realize they won't, bring it to an end.

When you find yourself in a relationship that needs to be terminated, and you're having difficulty doing so, ask yourself the following questions:

1. What is the worst thing that could happen if I end a bad relationship?
2. What is the best thing that could happen if I end a bad relationship?
3. Can I deal with the worst thing that could happen? If I can, then I should end a bad relationship.

It is good to examine your relationships regularly to make sure that they are beneficial for you and that your life is being beneficial to someone else. In every way possible, be at peace with others—even with those whom you think don't mean you any good and are out to get you. Never have ill-will towards anyone. If it gets too difficult to deal with some people, pronounce a benediction (final blessing) and move on. Continue to be cordial and kind and don't subject yourself to being abused by others.

Adolescence is a time of great uncertainty. You look for stability and security wherever you can find it. Your parents are on your last nerve many times, and your siblings are getting there quickly. You may feel at times that you don't fit in anywhere. You are very vulnerable during this time. Try not to misinterpret what is actually going on. Don't isolate yourself from those who love you. If you have difficulty with members in your immediate family, branch out to extended family members. Your blood relatives will be there for you through the turbulence of adolescent years. You will find someone to click with if you just keep searching. Some adjustments may have to be made as to how family members relate to one another, but don't give up on having meaningful relationships with family members.

Your mentoring cell group is also a positive peer group where you are accepted for who you are and held accountable for what you do.

Questions

1. Are you applying peer pressure or are you responding to peer pressure?

2. What friends or famous people influence you?

3. What do you give and what do you receive from your peer group?

4. Does your peer group revolve around one person?

5. Do you think about the character of your friends?

6. Do you compromise your convictions to be included in a group or do you have the strength of character to stand alone when necessary?

7. Do you have the right enemies?

8. Do you know any terrorists or temptresses?

9. Do you need to move out of any unhealthy relationships?

10. As much as possible, are you at peace with others?

Mother Wit

True friendship is like sound health, the value of it is seldom known until it be lost. CHARLES CALEB COLTON

I don't know the key to success, but the key to failure is trying to please everybody. BILL COSBY

Friendship demands the ability to do without it. RALPH WALDO EMERSON

The greatest good you can do for another is not just to share your riches, but to reveal to him his own. ANONYMOUS

Every man has a mob self and an individual self, in varying proportions. D. H. LAWRENCE

If a man does not keep pace with his companions, perhaps it is because he hears a different drummer. Let him step to the music which he hears, however measured or far away. HENRY DAVID THOREAU

If you expect somebody else to guide you, you'll be lost. JAMES EARL JONES

Social workers point to an enormous psychological problem in our society: many young people have never experienced a deep emotional attachment to anyone. They do not know how to love and be loved. The need to be loved translates itself into the need to belong to someone or something. Driven by that need, these young people become the victims of cults, of peer pressure of fads, in short, of any mass movement at hand. They will do anything to belong. ALBERT LALONDE

You are beautiful; but learn to work,
for you cannot eat your beauty.

Congo

20
Not Your Traditional Beauty
(appreciating your physical design)

$\sim$

W hen I was an adolescent I danced to a popular song whose lyrics detailed a woman's physical dimensions, personal demeanor and style of dress. If a girl was referred to as a "brick house," you knew her measurements right away—36-24-36 (bust, waist and hips)—or somewhere close to that. These dimensions were considered the standard for a beautiful, hourglass shape. If you had them, you were considered stacked. If you didn't, then, oh well.

I have had these dimensions before—but not at the same time. When my waist was 24 inches, my bust and hips weren't 36. When my bust and hips were 36 inches, my waist was no longer 24. Physically, I've never been stacked as a traditional beautiful. Oh well. There are more people like me who do not measure up to this standard than ones who do. Unfortunately, this reality has not sobered those who wish for ideals or soothed those who are not traditionally beautiful. Magazines, movies and music all help to promote this image myth. How unfortunate!

The *not your traditional beauty* comes from all walks of life. She is degreed (college-educated), and un-degreed (not college educated). She is Black, White, Latina, African, Asian and from every other part of the world. She is gifted, talented, intelligent, and beautiful—and not just beautiful in her own way, either. She is beautiful, period! But with all of her wonderful attributes, she still faces a lot of challenges in her professional and personal life. We live in a very visual society where image means a great deal. If a girl doesn't fit the accepted image, her way may be difficult. It doesn't have to be, but it usually is. Standards have been set and there is little appreciation for anything that goes against the grain. Fortunately, some of the images are being challenged. But the idols haven't completely been brought down yet.

The *not your traditional beauty* does not fit the standard and is not always accepted and appreciated. At work and at school, she may be the victim of blatant discrimination (the in-your-face type of unfair treatment), or she may be subjected to covert discrimination (the secret, under-cover, not-so-easily detected type). If she is ample and full-bodied, she may be considered lazy, unhealthy and unproductive. Studies indicate that she is less likely to be offered an interview. If hired, she makes less money than someone who has an average build. She is also less likely to be promoted. If the *not your traditional beauty* is thin, she may be considered insecure, inept, unstable and unqualified. People will not always come out and tell you what they think of you so it is important for you to understand how others prejudge you based on your appearance. You need some understanding in order to intelligently handle your situations.

There are also certain challenges in her personal life. She will receive compliments on her personality, spirit, and intellect, but not on her physical beauty. She may also be denied any expression of affection and treated like one of the gang at all times. Statements such as, "She's nice," "She has a nice personality," "She is a good friend," "I can really talk to her," "She's going to make someone a good wife," and "I'd ask her out, but she's just not my type," are some of the statements said about her. Do any of these sound familiar? The *not your traditional beauty* has heard several, if not all of these statements. At first they sound harmless, but a closer listen reveals something else.

When you first read these statements, they sound like compliments, don't they? But placed in the context of someone who doesn't receive very many calls, hasn't been asked out for many dates, and has little to no prospects for a date to the junior or senior prom, these statements are serious blows to the self-esteem. These seemingly innocent remarks are filtered through her experience and translated as "I'm not attractive," "Nobody wants to be seen with me," "I'll never be asked out," and "What's wrong with me?" The *not your traditional beauty* is challenged. Will she become bitter, or will she become better? What to do? How to feel? If you are a *not your traditional beauty*, or if you know a *not your traditional beauty*, consider the following three points and share them with a friend:

1. Approve of yourself. Is your body performing for you? You might not look like a fashion model, but does your body serve you well? Does it do what it is supposed to do? As one who travels a lot, I have a simple motto. "Go light." Don't carry excess baggage. It's not worth the weight. I apply this to weight as well. If your weight is aiding you, and you need it to be all that you can be, then keep it. If it is in excess and not serving you, get rid of it. Food satisfies many needs. We derive comfort from eating. If you overeat, know why you do it. If you don't eat enough, understand this also. Keep track of how often you eat in a day. What purpose does eating serve you?

2. Appreciate yourself. For your body type, age and heredity, are your healthy? Consider your anatomy. We are all endowed differently. Over the years I have put on some weight. People

171

in my hometown comment on my weight and size now because when I was growing up I was all arms and legs, skinny and bony. I knew that one day I would fill out because I have a medium build with broad shoulders. I'm not surprised at my size now. I think I look healthier. I know that I am stronger.

3. Applaud yourself. Compliment yourself. Stay positive. Attitude is everything. Wear a positive attitude at all times. It is the beginning of a very attractive appearance.

Whether we like it or not, physical appearance plays a major role in how people perceive and receive us. Appearance does matter. There are some things that all beauties should consider regarding appearance. Consider the following:

1. Take care of your personal self. Be clean—bathe, shower and use the proper anti-perspirant, powder, oils and lotions for your skin type.

2. Make sure that your hands, fingernails and teeth are always clean and presentable.

3. Make certain that your foundation is firm. Wear the proper undergarments for the proper coverage and support. No bikini panty lines, please. No designs that can be seen through your skirt, shorts or slacks.

4. Wear quality fabrics. A good fit and fine fabric is always very attractive.

5. Wear your size. Don't wear clothes that are too small or too big.

6. Make exercise a part of your life. Exercise gives you a glow. Get healthy.

7. Your hair must be there. Keep it together, looking good, touched up, clean and styled.

8. Use make-up as an accent not an accident. Enhance your natural beauty.

If you are a *not your traditional beauty* who is ample and full-bodied, here are some things you should consider when dressing:

1. Dress up and not down. No jogging suits, unless you're jogging. No baggy clothes. Baggy looks bigger.

2. Be careful of patterns and designs. Be aware of how you look from all sides.

3. You do have a shape. Wear clothes that proportion your shape.

Back in the day, young ladies who had ample shapes had few choices when shopping. Clothes were usually purchased in the misses' and women's sections and the styles were not contemporary. Today, several retailers have launched clothing lines for full-bodied adolescents. Invest in quality attire. You're worth it. Cheap clothes look cheap.

If you are a *not your traditional beauty* who is thin, consider these suggestions when dressing.

1. Don't dress too skimpily. Most trends and fads are directed at your body size. Stay modest and chaste in your dress regardless of what's on a New York runway. Don't wear underwear as outerwear.

2. Wear clothes that are feminine. Stay away from the unisex look. Go for the soft, feminine, flowing look in sportswear,

173

casual wear and formal wear.

If you are the traditional beauty in physical design, there are some things you should consider also.

1. Don't dress provocatively. Be chaste and modest. Make sure that you are not advertising. Don't bring attention to your endowment—stay away from low-cut, tight tops, mid-riff shirts, and too tight slacks.

2. Don't depend on your looks. Make sure that you are a lady of substance. There is much more to you than what is visible to the eye.

3. Beauty fades. Make sure that you spend time getting your mind and heart together.

Lastly, if you are a *not your traditional beauty* who does not receive many phone calls or dates, faint not. Consider the following:

1. Don't start the blame game. Stop asking what is wrong with you. There is not necessarily anything wrong with you. What's wrong with the gentlemen who don't ask you out?

2. Start celebrating what's right with you—all of your gifts, skills and talents.

3. Work on being a complete person. Enter a relationship as a whole person, able to contribute to the relationship and complement another person.

4. Get your personal act together—personally, emotionally spiritually and academically. A relationship amplifies problems. Deal with any severe problems and struggles you are having before you enter a relationship. A boyfriend is not a savior.

5. You may be ready for a date, but your potential date is not ready yet. Be patient. Don't settle.

6. Accept the fact that it may not be your season to date. Be content being single.

7. Don't compromise your character or body to get a date.

8. Don't dismiss someone that you find unattractive.

9. Don't be afraid to date someone with a different body type than you.

People are attracted to people who are attractive. People who are going somewhere are the people who are pursued. Have direction in your life because you are going somewhere, not just to attract a date. If you attract a man based only on how you look, you are operating on shaky ground. External beauty fades and there is always going to be somebody who looks a little better than you, is shaped a little better and has a better package. Don't base your attractiveness on your outside appearance alone. Be balanced. Become attractive on the inside and outside. Be able to carry on a conversation.

People are interested in people who are interesting. Appearance is important, but don't spend more time on your appearance than on your personality. Work on your personality so that it is pleasant and strong so that you will not have to advertise who you are through your dress. Make certain that you are putting something in your head and in your heart. Get a good education and learn some valuable life skills.

Questions

1. Do you consider yourself a traditional beauty?

2. In what ways do you feel that you are untraditionally beautiful?

3. How is the "image myth" promoted in today's society?

4. Have you ever been mistreated because of your physical characteristics?

5. Do you have biased feelings toward girls based on their appearance?

6. What statements have you heard made about the *not your traditional beauty*?

7. If you overeat, do you know why?

8. As time passes, are you growing bitter or better?

9. Of all of the tips given, which are the most helpful or most important for you right now?

Mother Wit

To put it bluntly, I seem to be a whole superstructure with no foundation. But I'm working on the foundation.
MARILYN MONROE

A Satin Doll is a woman who is as pretty on the inside as she is on the outside. DUKE ELLINGTON

Let us act on what we have, since we have not what we wish.
CARDINAL NEWMAN

Do not wish to be anything but what you are, and try to be that perfectly. UNKNOWN

From birth to 18, a girl needs good parents. From 18 to 35, she needs good looks. From 35 to 55 good personality. From 55 on, she needs good cash. I'm saving my money.
SOPHIE TUCKER

There are no ugly women, only lazy ones.
HELENA RUBENSTEIN

Women who set a low value on themselves make life hard for all women. NELLIE MCCLUNG

It is amazing how complete is the delusion that beauty is goodness. LEO TOLSTOY

Beauty without expression tires. RALPH WALDO EMERSON

Do you love me because I am beautiful or am I beautiful because you love me? OSCAR HAMMERSTEIN, II

Pretty can only get prettier,
but beauty compounds itself.

J. Kennedy Ellington

21
Form and Fashion
(DWI: dressing with instructions)

Finished or frayed, hot pants (a.k.a. Daisy Dukes) were the rage when I was a teenager. They were available in solids, prints, and in every color and fabric from cotton denim to those twins poly and ester (polyester). Shorts so short that you had to stoop to pick up what you dropped, was a must-have. A two-lyric popular song added to the craze. I admit I had a few pair. Yes, I did. And wore them too. Yes, I did. Skinny legs and all. It was hot pants in the summertime and hip-huggers in the winter. Now, there is nothing wrong with fashion as long as fashion is not wrong. But, when shorts are so short that a warning sign is required before you are viewed from behind, fashion has gone wrong. Trust me, mine were not that short.

When fashion creates an unsafe environment, then the freedom to choose what you wear must be challenged. Some fabrics were not intended for outer wear. The very nature of the material suggests intimacy. Not all dress that is permissible, is necessarily profitable. When what you wear causes you potential danger, you must use discretion and caution. It is reported that many rapes and abuse of women are the results of men being exposed to pornography. Revealing, suggestive clothing can be compared to wardrobe pornography—some clothing is legal to wear but immoral to wear. Young ladies must be careful not to market their sexuality through their dress. Do not underestimate a young man's imagination, especially if you give him a lot to work with.

All dress is intentional. We think and decide what to put on every day. Our dress sends out messages loudly and clearly. We must be careful that our unspoken signals support what we are saying. There is a trend to wear foundation wear as outerwear. Don't follow it. Be modest in your dress. Don't come out looking like you didn't finish getting dressed with buttons unbuttoned, zippers unzipped, house shoes on, scarves and rags on your head, etc. Your clothes should cover you so that there is something left for people to imagine about you. I am always embarrassed when I see ladies in clothes that outline their shapes and leave nothing to the imagination.

The clothes you wear tell a lot about how you feel about yourself. A girl has to consider how she wants to be perceived by others. It is important that you wear clothes that show others that you feel good about yourself. I enjoy dressing. I have developed a habit of wearing the clothes that make me feel my best on days when I may not feel so good. I use my wardrobe to brighten up my mood. I make it a habit to look good, smell good and feel that greatness is upon me.

For all types of beauties, there are some garments that you should have in your closet at all times. A black skirt, a white blouse, a black dress, a white dress, camisoles, a full slip, a half slip, a panty-girdle and black shoes are considered staples (wardrobe essentials). Plan to build your wardrobe gradually. When I started working, I purchased one item that I could afford from each paycheck. I saved for more expensive items, such as nice dresses, suits or jackets. I gradually built a wardrobe. I didn't go out and buy a lot of items of poor quality. I purchased classic designs that I could wear for several years.

Find out what colors and styles look best on you and coordinate your accessories.

There are so many different gifts of physical endowment (shapes). Some of us don't have the form (shape) for some of the fashions. Understand your body type. Don't wear clothes that accentuate (stress and emphasize) your endowment. Do not wear tight knit tops on large busts or spandex stretch pants on wide hips without a blouse to cover the hips. Try on clothes before you buy them. Do not trust the size on the label. In some cases the label lied because one size does not fit all. Yes, you have the right to wear what you pay for. But, remember every body can't wear everything.

Questions

1. How would you describe your style of dress?

2. How do you feel about pornography?

3. Do you enjoy giving a man's imagination a lot to work with?

4. How much time do you take trying to decide what to wear each day?

5. Do you enjoy dressing?

6. What is the benefit of purchasing a "classic design"?

7. Do you know what colors and types of clothes look good on you?

8. Do you know how to coordinate your accessories?

9. What messages are you sending with the way you dress?

10. Does the way you dress correspond with what you say?

11. If you have a loving, caring, goin'-on dad, which articles of clothing would he delete from your closet?

12. Do you have any clothing that is legal to wear but immoral to wear?

Mother Wit

Fashions fade—style is eternal. YVES SAINT LAURENT

All women's dresses are merely variations on the eternal struggle between the admitted desire to dress and the unadmitted desire to undress. LIN YUTANG

Some women just don't know how great they really are. They come to us all vogue outside and vague on the inside. MARY KAY ASH

Beauty comes in all size—not just size 5. ROSEANNE BARR ARNOLD

There is new strength, repose of mind, and inspiration in fresh apparel. ELLA WHEELER WILCOX

Women dress alike all over the world: they dress to be annoying to other women. ELSA SCHIAPARELLI

The well dressed man is he whose clothes you never notice. W. SOMERSET MAUGHAM

A love of fashion makes the economy go round. LIZ TILBERIS

Fashion can be bought. Style one must possess. EDNA WOOLMAN CHASE

Every generation laughs at the old fashions, but follows religiously the new. HENRY DAVID THOREAU

It is natural for a man to woo a woman, not for a woman to woo a man: the loser seeks what he has lost (the rib).
The Talmud

22
Stop the Pursuit!
(controlling your passions)

~~~

Do you remember team sports on the school playground? Captains were chosen, usually by the teacher, and then the captains proceeded to select their teams. It always felt good to be picked early. It felt even better to have been chosen first. But nothing felt worse than to be assigned to a team or not chosen at all.

We never grow out of the need to be chosen, to feel selected, to be asked. While society has retreated to girls asking boys out and even to women proposing to men, I believe that if we are really honest about it, women still prefer to be chosen. There is something within a man that needs to know that he is the initiator. And there is something within a woman that must know that she is sought after. Being forward seems like a lot of fun at first, but it gets frustrating fast.

I remember vividly my first real boyfriend and the first time he was allowed to come to my house to see me. We lived five country miles apart. We did not even attend the same school. A mutual friend gave him a picture of me. He sent me his picture and asked for my phone number. Through our friend, I sent the number. We talked on the telephone for months before he asked my mother if he could come to the house to see me. I was courted, which is fast becoming a dying art. Many telephone calls and letters preceded the face-to-face encounter. Whenever he called, he always respected my mother by talking to her before asking to speak to me. He had a relationship with her as well, which served him nicely. Because of their relationship, whenever I missed a call, she was sure to deliver the message.

The big day finally came. My first male visitor. My mother gave him a specific time to arrive and a specific time to leave. He and I both knew that he had better stick to her schedule because my Mama didn't take no mess! He arrived on time—a perfect gentleman—mannerable, well-dressed and with a perfectly-maintained 'fro (Afro). I was excited and nervous at the same time.

After the preliminary greeting and some small talk with my mother, we spent the remainder of our "hour" together finally talking face-to-face. The hour came and went so quickly, and then he was off as he had arrived, to hitchhike a ride back home. (We called this "thumbing").

I was very impressed with my first boyfriend. He was smart, handsome, and most of all, wise. He chose me to be his girlfriend. He sought me out. He could have picked somebody else. But he risked life and limb, hitchhiking, to come and see me.

While I did not give him my heart, he certainly captured a special place there. He was the standard by which other boyfriends were compared. I still have very fond memories of him. I was fortunate. My first boyfriend was a good one. He came from a good family. He had sisters. He had some understanding about what a woman is like, what she likes and the sacrifices that a man must be willing to make on her behalf. I was most fortunate because I had a mother who talked to me.

My mother told me what a man is like, what a man likes and what sacrifices are acceptable for a young lady to make for the man she likes. I had some guidelines about relationships before I ever had one. The talks my mother had with me included some very specific advice. There were some do's and do not's.

1. Do not make the initial phone call to a boy. Do return his call, but do not make the first call.

2. Do not dominate the conversation. Be a good listener. Let the young man do most of the talking. Learn as much as you can about him from him.

3. Do not volunteer information that is not being asked for. Keep the young man interested and inquiring.

4. Be willing to wait for what you want. Have some non-negotiables and some negotiables based upon established criteria. Characteristics that are non-negotiable include a good work ethic; good morals, integrity and character; and respect for you as an equal. You can negotiate on his physical appearance—he doesn't have to be tall, dark and handsome with an athletic build. If he's worthy, he will be willing to meet your reasonable demands. Don't sell yourself cheaply. Know your worth and value. If you hold out for better treatment, you will eventually receive it.

5. Do not enter a relationship thinking that you can change another person. Do not think that you can raise a half-grown young man. Don't try and replace his Mama! If he is consistently late, rude and disrespectful, he ain't cute! Remember, you are not desperate. You wouldn't take such behavior from a sister-friend, don't tolerate it from a brother-friend.

I heard a saying when I was coming up that I will never forget. *Why buy the cow when the milk is free?* In a nutshell, this saying had to do with self-respect and self-worth. Remember, if you sell yourself cheaply, you cannot raise the price later.

As a young woman, you have tremendous influence. You can affect a brother's behavior like no one else can. Practice self-restraint, saying no and meaning NO! Use your influence to make the brother better.

Today, you are challenged to pursue what you want. It is a relentless, endless exercise. It's also all up in your face. Videos, CDs, tapes, movies, books—everywhere you turn, you are faced with suggestions on how-to "jump on that." Equal opportunity has been carried to every arena of life. But this practice is a no-win situation for you. What is portrayed on TV, video, movies and other types of media is not real. Don't fall for it.

Men are initiators and women are responders. There are big problems when you reverse roles. It may seem like fun at first, but a real man has to make a conquest. He may not be loud and aggressive with it, but he must conquer according to his personality. The words from the Talmud remind us of this.

It is natural for a man to woo a woman, not for a woman to woo a man: the loser seeks what he has lost (the rib).

A woman can be a lot of things. A woman can do a lot of things. But a woman can never be a man. You can out-think him. You can out-talk him. But you can't out-man a man. When a woman acts like a man, she sets herself up for big disappointment.

Concerning pursuit, what part of "stop" don't you understand?

Questions

1. Are you good at controlling your passions?

2. Tell the truth. Do you enjoy being chosen?

3. Do you remember your first boyfriend?

4. What criteria do you have for the men you will date?

5. What would a man have to do to impress you?

6. Have you learned how to be a good listener?

7. Have you ever started watching a movie and turned it off or left when you decided that it was inappropriate?

8. What do you do when you have problems controlling your passions?

9. What are some consequences of not controlling your passions?

10. On a scale of 1 to 10 with 10 being the greatest, how good are you at controlling your passions?

Circle one: 1   2   3   4   5   6   7   8   9   10

Mother Wit

I always knew that fury was my natural enemy. It clotted my blood and clogged my pores. It literally blinded me so that I lost my peripheral vision. MAYA ANGELOU

Nothing will do me any good unless I learn to control this body of mine. ALICE NELSON DUNBAR

We should employ our passions in the service of life, not spend life in the service of our passions. RICHARD STEELE

A man without self-control is as defenseless as a city with broken-down walls. KING SOLOMON

The heart has its reasons which reason knows nothing of. BLAISE PASCAL

How shall I be able to rule over others when I have not full power and command over myself? RABELAIS

Don't compromise yourself. You are all you've got. JANIS JOPLIN

Keep thy heart with all diligence for out of it are the issues of life. KING SOLOMON

Above all else, guard your affections. For they influence everything else in our life. KING SOLOMON

r - e- s - p - e- c - t. Find out what it means to me. ARETHA FRANKLIN

23
The Man:
A Woman's Long-Term Project
(matters of the heart)

She will not hinder him but help him all her life.
LEMUEL'S MOTHER

When I was growing up, I had several hobbies. Singing was chief among them. I don't remember a time when I didn't sing. It began as a hobby—something that I liked to do as a favorite pastime—and developed into my life's vocation. Along with music, I enjoyed doing other things. I remember collecting S & H Green Stamps, acquiring charms for my charm bracelet, crocheting blankets and weaving gum wrapper chains, to name a few. Each of these hobbies required a long-term commitment of time, energy and interest.

The stamps were collected at grocery stores and pasted in little booklets that were sent in to receive merchandise from a gift catalogue. I received my charms as birthday gifts or at Christmas as exchange presents from my friends. Little by little, my skeins of yarn turned into blankets that I hoped to use for my children one day. And the completion of the gum wrapper chains depended on how much gum I chewed or could get someone else to chew. None of my hobbies were completed instantly. They were mostly long-term projects, which required diligence, care and some deliberate work.

I became interested in some of my hobbies as a result of watching my sisters, Linda and Anita. I was curious about what they were interested in and wanted to do what they did. I watched them move from one project to another until finally, they turned from making things with their hands to matters of the heart.

I was around 7 or 8 when I became aware of my older sisters' interest in the opposite sex. I remember them talking on the telephone, going out on dates and having company at the house. But since my sisters are 9 and 7 years older than I am, I was not in on the details of their conversations. From what I observed, though, boyfriends could be delightful and they could be difficult. I knew that boys were different because I have brothers. But just how different they were, I didn't realize until I experienced my own affairs of the heart.

A man is not a woman, was not intended to be a woman and therefore can never be a woman. His ways are not her ways, neither are his thoughts her thoughts. Physically, hormonally and emotionally, he is different. It is not a matter of conditioning. It is a matter of biology. And because he is different biologically, he responds with a different behavior. He acts the way he acts because he thinks the way he thinks (remember?). This fundamental truth will help you understand what seems incomprehensible. He does not act the way a woman thinks he should act. He acts the way a man thinks he should act and therefore must be approached from an understanding of his perspective. The woman who wants to achieve any measure of success in the area of male-female relations must be willing to understand and appreciate the differences. Gaining this understanding and appreciation does not happen overnight. It is a process.

A man is a woman's long-term project. He represents an intensive course of study which requires commitment, sensitivity and diligence. He is not a project for the faint at heart. To deal successfully with a man, there must be a commitment to staying with what you start, a commitment to study and learning. It is not instantaneous. It is a process. You understand a man better by and by.

When you deal with a man, you go to school. While every individual is unique and has distinct characteristics, there are some features common to the male species. Dealing with men presents you with tremendous opportunities for growth. Nothing grows you like matters of the heart. The more you learn, the more there is to know. Here are a few things that you can look forward to when you deal with a man. Let's go to school.

1. His actions are based upon his thoughts. To be successful, the first thing you must do is to get in on his viewpoint. You must understand his mindset. Understanding a male's point of view will require some flexibility. Note: I said *flexibility*, not compromise. You are not to compromise your principles (virtue and purity) in trying to be understanding. Remember your non-negotiables. There should be some flexibility. You should be open to different approaches and ways of doing things. To effectively deal with a man, you must be willing to adjust your learning and working styles. Answer the following questions: How differently can something be done? What is your preferred way? Consider the other ways as viable alternatives. Your preferred way will probably not be the way he does things.

2. Because a wise man wants a woman who is cautious and who is not too available, he will be cautious in his pursuit.

Women often interpret this as being slow. His caution is a safeguard. He is just trying to be sure. He doesn't want to be hurt. No man wants a woman who is too easy. He wants to have the thrill of initiative and conquest. Don't always be available to receive his phone call.

3. Because he thinks that there is more to a woman, he never fully reveals himself. He is usually on reserve. What you see is not what you get. Men are intrigued by the feminine mystique—women who don't bare their souls. They enjoy the challenge of trying to figure you out. Because he likes the game of discovery, expect him not to bare his soul to you.

4. A question requires an answer, not an explanation. Most men like to problem-solve alone and usually verbalize only the bottom line, whereas women usually answer six questions when delivering information (what, when, why, how, where and who). Don't sweat the details. Accept the bottom line and be patient. When he retells the story, which he will, he will fill it out with more information. Wait on him.

5. Repetitive questioning equals a challenge. In order to win, he will retreat. A man is not interested in going tit-for-tat verbally with a woman. A smart man knows that a woman can think faster, talk faster and respond quicker than he can, therefore his strategy is silence.

6. Demonstration equals verbalization. A man feels that he can show you better than he can tell you, especially if it involves romantic feelings. Study his ways of communicating and accept them. Don't demand that he speak the way that you speak.

There are several skills that you will acquire or enhance when you work on a man as your long-term project.

1. You will learn how to hear what has not been said. Your hearing will be sharpened.

2. You will learn to be understanding when things are not clearly understandable. You will gain patience.

3. You will learn how to see what isn't there. Your vision will be enhanced.

4. You will expand your vocabulary because you will learn how to repeat yourself without repeating yourself (saying the same things over and over in very creative ways).

Male-female relationships should not be entered into lightly or unadvisedly. The decision to become related in any way with a man other than friendship should be carefully considered. Matters of the heart are not passive activities, nor are they spectator sports. They require heart commitments and uncover our true intentions. A man as a long-term project requires a commitment to using your strengths to benefit someone else without any expectation of something in return. Your only motivation must be to help someone else be all that he can be. You must decide early on if you are willing to make such an investment. Make sure that you have something to work with, because a relationship is costly.

I am glad that I had the opportunity to know my father-in-law. We disagreed on a lot of things, mostly because he was a master of disagreement, but I learned a lot about my husband from spending time with him. The greatest compliment he ever paid me was in regards to his son. He said, "Thank you for what you've done for my son." He knew that I had taken on a project. And if I had it to do over, I'd do it again.

Questions

1. Do you have any brothers? If so, what have you learned from them? If not, how have you learned about boys?

2. Why should some young ladies wait until they are older before they get serious about men?

3. Do you want to date a bunch of men or do you want to take on one good project?

4. Do you feel that you understand the male viewpoint?

5. What is the difference between flexibility and compromise?

6. Are you available to the next man who wants to talk?

7. Do you disregard men who are considered slow?

8. Do you understand what the feminine mystique is?

9. What do you know about male-female relationships?

10. As a result of this lesson, how do you feel about dating, going steady or marriage?

11. Do you know an older, wiser woman who can help you understand men?

Mother Wit

One of the things being in politics has taught me is that men are not a reasoned or reasonable sex.
MARGARET THATCHER

We can finally say that we're in love.
WHITNEY HOUSTON AND BOBBY BROWN

The average girl would rather have beauty than brains because she knows the average man can see much better than he can think. LADIES HOME JOURNAL

Mama seemed to do only what my father wanted, and yet we lived the way my mother wanted us to live. LILLIAN HELLMAN

Outward beauty is not enough; to be attractive a woman must. . . [use] words, wit, playfulness, sweet-talk and laughter to transcend the gifts of Nature. PETRONIUS

Social science affirms that a woman's place in society marks the level of civilization. ELIZABETH CADY STANTON

My family keeps me centered. They tell me when I need to turn the dial down. EARL G. GRAVES

Our job is to put the man back into manhood.
NATHANIEL GOLDSTON

Teach a wise man, and he will be the wiser; teach a good man, and he will learn more. KING SOLOMON

Momma seemed to do only what my father wanted, and yet we lived the way my mother wanted us to live.

Lillian Hellman

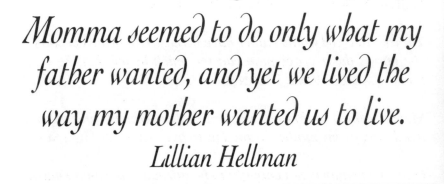

Part V

Claiming Wisdom and Climbing Higher

The foolish and wicked practice of profane cursing and swearing is a vice so mean and low that every person of sense and character detests and despises it
George Washington

24
Profanity is NOT a Punctuation Remark!
(disdaining bad language)

Have you ever had your mouth washed out with soap? Has anyone ever threatened to wash your mouth out with soap? I have not had the experience first-hand, but I am told by a very reliable source (my daughter, Ashley) that Dove is bitter, that it burns and that it leaves a very disgusting aftertaste.

I performed the soap mouth-wash procedure only once and don't fully remember that instance, but when I mentioned the focus of this chapter to Ashley, she recalled the incident with all of the details. It had served its purpose.

Ashley's experience with a soap mouth-wash was the result of her engaging in an adolescent's favorite pastime—name-calling. In a moment of frustration, she called her brother an idiot. Now, you may be thinking, "That wasn't all that bad." I admit that she could have said much worse. But, the soap mouth-wash served as the needed inspiration for her to clean up her vocal act. She had been given fair warning regarding this pastime, as well as the inappropriateness of other remarks, before she met the mouth-washing consequences.

Let me remind you that words are powerful. They have the power to heal and to hurt. They are audible thoughts, verbalized beliefs that cannot go unchecked. Ashley, in a moment of frustration, hurt her brother. And she used words as her weapon.

Name-calling says more about the person doing the calling than the person being called. The words we use tell a lot about us. We utter what is within us. Out of the abundance of our hearts, we speak words. Whether pure or profane, our words show what's in our hearts. The person using foul language knows its meaning and the intention behind its usage. The choice of words is deliberate.

Your words will either defend you or condemn you. Pleasant, pure words defend your cause, whereas profanity condemns you, placing you at a disadvantage before there's an opportunity to really get to know you.

In my day, the come-back response to being called out of your name was *it takes one to know one*. What happened next usually depended upon the motive and mood of the initial commentator. This come-back response could bring the contest to an end, or it could be the catalyst for an all-out altercation (physical fight). Usually, the person dishing it out couldn't take it, and wanted to become violent.

Cursing always scared me. I have witnessed too many arguments that started off in jest—as just an exchange of a few words and then escalated to full-blown fist fights. Verbal banter is dangerous because you can't predict the reaction of the other person. You don't know what your remarks will trigger.

I knew my share of notorious cursers and I tried to avoid them. They weren't congratulated or celebrated for their filthy mouths. Instead, they were usually regarded as people you didn't want to be around and to watch out for. You didn't want to get caught in the cross-fire of their spewing forth. It is hard to predict what words will incite.

Sometimes foul language is used to start a fight. But there are other reasons too. Poor excuses for using profane language include:

1. You were mad.
2. It just came out.
3. Everybody curses.

Using profane language is one of the earliest ways people try to act grown. What a person lacks in age, she tries to make up for in language. Some people want to appear schooled in the street tradition. This desire to sound informed is what motivates the use of profanity—young girls want to sound savvy. Nobody wants to sound naive.

Profanity is also used for its shock value—littered throughout sentences as coarse interjections that show excitement or emotion, or as vulgar punctuation marks when the feelings are not as strong. But profanity is not a punctuation remark! It doesn't give closure to a thought as does a period. It doesn't connect a train of thought as does a comma, semi-colon or colon. Nor does it ask a question that demands an answer. Profanity raises questions that you would rather not answer, such as your competence, couth and ability to apply intelligence. It is a subliterate, unimaginative, uncreative, base, gutter utterance. It adds nothing significant to the conversation. Should you omit the cursing, you would lose none of the meaning of the statement. Profanity is a feeble attempt to sound profound but accomplishes only what is profane. It handicaps your conversation, cripples your integrity and clouds your morality.

Nobody likes to get checked. But sometimes it is critically necessary. Consider this talk on profanity as you would a periodic check-up at a dentist office. Just as a thorough mouth examination is a good indication of your overall health, this close look at your vocabulary reveals what's in your heart. Are you in need of some inspiration to clean up your vocabulary?

Questions

1. Do you come from a cursing environment?

2. Do you curse? Why or why not?

3. What is your perception of those who curse?

4. Can you give an example that confirms the fact that words are powerful?

5. How do your words reflect what is in your heart?

6. Have your words ever gotten you into a fight?

7. Can you think of any good reason to use profanity?

8. What practical steps do you recommend for those who need to clean up their language?

Mother Wit

The foolish and wicked practice of profane cursing and swearing is a vice so mean and low that every person of sense and character detests and despises it. GEORGE WASHINGTON

Be careful of your thoughts; they may become words at any moment. IARA GASSEN

People fighting their aloneness will do almost anything to avoid silence. MYRTLE BARKER

Kind words are like honey—enjoyable and healthful. KING SOLOMON

Violence of language leads to violence of action. Angry men seldom fight if their tongues do not lead the fray. CHARLES V. ROMAN

Self-control means controlling the tongue! A quick retort can ruin everything. KING SOLOMON

Language is the apparel in which your thoughts parade before the public. Never clothe them in vulgar or shoddy attire. GEORGE CRANE

I'm the son of a minister and I just can't tell dirty jokes. Even if I could, I wouldn't. You can be funny without cursing and doing sex jokes. SINBAD

Thousands of people can speak at least two languages—English and profanity. JOE CLARK

Accumulating money is so easy, I'm surprised more people aren't rich. That's the way money works. The important thing is not how much money a person makes, it is what he does with it that matters.

A.P. Gaston

25
Healthy Attitudes About Money
(to be secured, saved, shared and spent)

I formed many attitudes about money at an early age. Much of what I do now as it relates to handling money can be directly traced to what I watched my mother and grandmother do when I was growing up. They taught me so many lessons, four of which I want to share with you.

I was about six years old when I was taught the value of a dollar (well, actually fifty cents). My mother took me uptown to the bank and opened a Christmas Savings Club account in my name. She made the initial deposit of five dollars to get me started and I made fifty-cent deposits weekly for the next ten months or so, somewhere from around late November to mid-October of the following year. If I deposited my fifty cents regularly and didn't withdraw any money before I was supposed to, the bank would make the last deposit. The bank's deposit was called interest. I also learned that there are two sides to compounding interest—the giving side and the receiving side. If the bank borrows from me, I'm on the receiving side; if I borrow from the bank, I'm on the giving side. When I put my money in the bank, I was on the receiving side.

At first I thought I was getting free money, but I later learned that interest is what depositors receive for allowing banks to use (borrow) their money while it is in the bank. I learned to be on the receiving side of compounding interest.

I also learned the power of systematic depositing. Little by little your money grows. Fifty cents a week grew to twenty-five dollars in a year. Ever since I was a child, I have believed that ***money is something to be saved.*** After saving for nearly a year (the goal was to save $25.00 a year), the bank sent me a notice in the mail stating that my goal had been reached and that I could come and withdraw my savings in time to shop for the holidays. We made the trip back uptown to make a withdrawal, but my mother didn't allow me to take out the whole amount. Five dollars stayed in as the deposit for the next year. From this I learned that ***money was something to be spent,*** but not to spend it all. I was taught to always have a reserve. To "not spend it all in one place" was also advice for the money that was withdrawn.

Learning to save money and learning to spend money was a lot easier than the third lesson—learning to share money. It was a hot summer afternoon and I needed twenty-five cents to buy a 16 oz. strawberry soda and a Three Musketeers candy bar. (Those were the good 'ole days.) I asked my mother if she had a quarter and she said she would look and see. While she was looking, my younger brother, Cuther, came in and asked her for a quarter also. She found one quarter and told us to buy the pop and candy and share it. I said that I had asked first and did not want to share. I wanted the whole bottle of pop and the whole candy bar to myself. She then said if I couldn't share half, I wouldn't have any. I chose to be stubborn and ended up with nothing. On that day, I learned that ***money is something to be shared.***

My grandmother is mostly responsible for my fourth

attitude. ***Money is something to be secured (earned).*** There were chores that I was expected to do as part of the family, and then there were things I could do *to make a little change* as she called it. She believed that everyone should keep a little something in their pockets. She was adamant about this with my older brothers. She often said, "Every man ought to have at least a dollar in his pocket at all times." She would get them up at the crack of dawn and have them pick blackberries, pass papers or do something to earn a little money. I washed windows, swept and mopped the floor or ran little errands to make my little change. Gramps taught me that money was something to be earned.

I learned as a child that money is important. It is something that you have to have in order to provide your needs and supply your wants. I have many memories of sitting at the kitchen table with my mother as she wrote out checks and money orders to pay bills. My job was to seal the envelopes and apply the stamps. Sometimes we walked across town and took payments in person. I sensed the pride she felt in taking care of business. She didn't like to owe anyone. I don't either.

My mother was not a very tall woman. She said she stood 5 feet, 7 ½ inches (I don't believe she was that tall). But after she paid her bills, she stood taller. The folded, paid receipts were precious possessions inside of her purse. She kept them until the next statement came, which showed that her payment had been received. She guarded them as if they were manumission papers that confirmed that she was a free woman. I love a receipt myself. I get very excited about receiving the titles to my cars, paid in full receipts and zero balance statements on credit cards.

There is nothing wrong with money. It is neither good nor bad. You should work hard and make all the money you honestly can. It is what you do with money, how you get money and how you feel about money that you have to be careful about. It is very important to have healthy attitudes about money. In the list below, note which ones you have.

Healthy Attitudes About Money

1. I will not let money control me.
2. I will not fall in love with money, because it cannot love me back.
3. I will not trust in money. It is not trustworthy. It can be here today and gone today.
4. I believe that it is important to save money.
5. I believe that it is important to spend money wisely.
6. I believe that it is important to share money.
7. I believe that I should pay my debts.
8. I believe that paying interest on something is not good stewardship. It's a waste of money.
9. I don't believe that money should be used to buy friendship.
10. I don't believe that money should be used to buy a relationship. I will not support a man.
11. I will not wear my wealth.
12. I will not flaunt my wealth.
13. I will not drive my wealth.
14. I will not try to impress others with money.

Money has a way of drawing people to you. People will come out of the woodwork if they think you have money. Be careful of your newfound popularity when you have a little cash or when people think you have a little cash. Settle some things in your mind before you are confronted with awkward situations.

I believe that the easiest way to handle situations is honestly and directly. Consider the following situations and the ways I suggest you handle them. You may decide to do otherwise, but make sure that you've thought it out thoroughly.

Situation	**Suggestion**
1. Loaning to Friends.	Don't

Don't ever loan money that you can't afford to lose. If you can afford to do without it, give it to them. If you can't afford it, say "no, I can't give you the money." This way you won't be upset if you are not paid back.

2. Borrowing from friends.   Don't

Don't bum from your friends. Don't strain a relationship. If you have a legitimate need, ask your friend to give you the money. If down the road you can pay it back, do so. If you don't ever pay it back, your friendship remains intact because repayment wasn't expected.

3. Co-signing.   Don't

Unless you can afford to pay for whatever you're being asked to co-sign for, don't take on the financial responsibility.

Your attitude toward money and what you do with it says a lot about what you think is important in life. Cultivate an attitude of gratitude concerning money. Be grateful for having your needs met. And if you should be blessed to receive more than you need, be truly thankful for the abundance. Wherever your treasure is, your heart will be there also.

Questions

1. Where did you get your attitudes toward handling money?

2. Do you love money?

3. Of saving, spending or sharing money, which is the hardest for you to do?

4. Who has taught you the importance of earning money?

5. Do you consider those in need when you think about money?

6. Do you owe anyone any money right now? What is your attitude toward anyone who owes you money?

7. Are you attracted to men who have money?

8. Of the "14 healthy attitudes", which are the hardest for you to have?

9. What do you plan to do to grow in those areas where you are financially weak?

10. Do you feel that you know the value of a dollar?

11. Do you have a savings account?

Mother Wit

I discovered I always have choices and sometimes it's only a choice of attitude. JUDITH M. KNOWLTON

If money is your hope for independence, you will never have it. The only real security that a man can have in this world is a reserve of knowledge, experience, and ability. HENRY FORD

Dishonest money brings grief to all the family, but hating bribes brings happiness. JEWISH PROVERB

Just as the rich rule the poor, so the borrower is servant to the lender. KING SOLOMON

It is poor judgment to countersign another's note, to become responsible for his debts. JEWISH PROVERB

Affluence separates people. Poverty knits 'em together. RAY CHARLES

Selfishness is the greatest curse of the human race. WILLIAM E. GLADSTONE

When money speaks, truth is silent. RUSSIAN PROVERB

Now if you want to know what a man is really like, take notice how he acts when he loses money. NEW ENGLAND PROVERB

Money is not required to buy one necessity of the soul. HENRY DAVID THOREAU

It wasn't raining when Noah built the ark. HOWARD RUFF

The key to success is to keep growing in all areas of life—mental, emotional, spiritual, as well as physical.

Julius Erving

26
How Grown is Grown?
(giving an account of yourself)

It is natural to want to be large and in charge. It is a universal desire. (A nature that we inherited. We are born in a rebellious state.) Few people really enjoy being told what to do. If you've ever been around children or remember being a child you know that among the very first words they say is the two letter word, NO! Whether voiced or acted out, "no" is clearly evident in us from the beginning. We come here trying to be grown.

"She ain't my Mama! She can't tell me what to do," and "Who she think she is, I don't have to listen to her" are expressions often made by young (adolescent, teen-age and young adult) women. They are not always verbally expressed. Some of us are too "polite" to say them, but they are expressed in other ways, specifically through our nonverbal vocabulary. We have thought them, or communicated in one of our other languages—the roll of the eye, the throw of the head, the grimace of the face, or the like. Or maybe you've had the following said of you—"She thinks she's grown." "She's too grown for me," or "I don't like being around *grown* kids."

Grown kids are oftentimes the result of early exposure to adult conversation. There was a time when children, girls and adolescents were not allowed to sit under grown folks. I was told to leave the room when my mother was visiting with her woman-friends. It was not proper to listen to grown folks' conversation then, and it's not proper now.

There is a danger in hearing mature conversations and lacking the maturity to comprehend their full meaning. You may hear the text (what is being said), but not understand the context (why it is being said) nor the subtext (what is meant by what is being said). Just because you can repeat the vocabulary with woman-like tone and inflection is not an indication that you fully comprehend the meaning.

When do you know you're grown? Or in other words, how grown is grown? Growth is a process, not a destination. No one completely arrives in this life. You may be mature in one area and lacking in another. There is always some area that can be improved upon. You grow as you acquire some knowledge, gain some experience and are wise enough to effectively apply what you know.

When you say, "she can't tell me anything," you're not acting grown. You can learn something from everyone. Don't limit your knowledge pool. The first step to becoming grown is to realize that you need to grow.

Grown is a state of being. It is not necessarily a number. I know a lot of people who have grown older but have failed to grow up. Being grown includes taking full responsibility for yourself—your decisions, actions, welfare and well-being. When you realize that you are your responsibility and there is no one to blame for your outcome, you are on your way to becoming grown.

I remember the day I realized tremendous growth. The day I became a woman. While there had been many events that marked stages of growth, development and maturity, such as menstruation, high school graduation, college graduation and my move to take my first teaching position, no event was as deciding or as defining as the one I'm about to share with you. In late August of 1979, my mother slipped into a state of consciousness where I could not enter. We had been there a few years before. Through many tears and prayers, I had petitioned the throne of God on my behalf—saying, "I'm not ready. Please God, don't take Mama." God was merciful. After nearly a month in a coma, she opened her eyes and began to speak. This time there were many similarities—the same hospital, the same doctors, the same medical condition—but the outcome was altogether different. I was still not ready to become a motherless child, but I was prepared. Nothing tested my maturity as did the loss of my earthly mother.

As my brother Matthew and I kept vigil alternating days with my mother at the hospital, I had lots of time to think. How prepared was I to carve out a life for myself? How well had I been taught? Or rather, how well had I learned? I wasn't ready to let her go, neither was I willing, but I had peace about it. I knew that I had been blessed to have been her daughter.

On September 8, 1979, my mother departed this life. I remember the day. I remember the hour. There were those who came to aid me and provide great comfort for me. But the reality that my anchor, the cloth from which I had been cut, was no longer a phone call or visit away, was a defining moment for me. It represented a major turning point in my life. I became my own responsibility completely.

You too will have a defining moment or moments in your life. Life will require you to make mature decisions. You want to be as prepared as you possibly can be. Listen and learn all that you can now from those who are sharing with you. Enjoy where you are now. This is a crucial stage in your life. Don't grow up too fast. Don't hurry through it. There is no returning to your childhood, adolescence or young adulthood. Once it is passed, it is over. You cannot go back.

I want to be like you when I grow up is a phrase that is often said as a compliment to someone who is admired and respected. My mother was and continues to be someone I want to be like. While I didn't always solicit the advice she offered, and there were times when I felt I knew as well as, if not better than she did, I am glad that she did not tolerate me acting grown as a kid.

How grown is grown? Grown is a state of being, where you make your own decisions, take responsibility for them and live with the consequences. Are you grown yet?

Questions

1. Do you consider yourself smart for your age?

2. If an older, wise woman shares wisdom with you, do you reject it if you have not experienced it?

3. When was the last time you thought you were grown and found out (the hard way) that you were not?

4. Rate your maturity in the following ways: Dealing with the opposite sex___ Staying away from negative influences___ Handling money___ Understanding and relating to others___ Valuing your education___

5. How have you matured in the last two years?

6. Name five specific things that you are doing to get more wisdom.

7. Do you realize that maturity is a life-long process of acquiring wisdom and applying it in our decisions?

Mother Wit

I believe that the sign of maturity is accepting deferred gratification. PEGGY CAHN

Character building begins in our infancy, and continues until death. ELEANOR ROOSEVELT

The key to success is to keep growing in all areas of life—mental, emotional, spiritual, as well as physical. JULIUS ERVING

It is better to be a poor but wise youth than to be an old and foolish king who refuses all advice. KING SOLOMON

A person isn't educated unless he has learned how little he already knows. THOMAS A. FLEMING

No one knows less than the person who knows it all. HUGH GLOSTER

Simply having children does not necessarily make a woman a mother. MARY FUTRELL

It takes twenty-one years to be twenty-one. REGGIE JACKSON

It's like this: when I was a child I spoke and thought and reasoned as a child does. But when I became a man my thoughts grew far beyond those of my childhood, and now I have put away the childish things. PAUL OF TARSUS

27
On Being a Woman of Color
(from personal experience)

R ecently, I decided to order an official copy of my birth certificate. I will need it a year from now to renew my passport. (I am quite pleased with myself for planning ahead and not waiting to the last minute to take care of business.) If you don't have copies of your vital documents, such as your Social Security card, your birth certificate, your immunization record, etc., I encourage you to get them. It's always better to have something and not need it, than to need something and not have it.

Since I was ordering a notarized copy of mine, I decided to order copies of my siblings' birth certificates as well. So far, I have received three of the seven I requested.

According to my certificate of live birth, I was born a female to a Negro mother. Two years prior to my birth, my brother Matthew was born a boy to a Colored mother according to his certificate of birth. And according to my brother Cuther's certificate two years after my birth, he was born a male to a Black mother. As for the certificates I haven't received yet, I suspect that on my older siblings' certificates my mother will be designated either Colored or Negro, and on my youngest brother's, she will be listed as Negro or Black. The color or ethnic designations given to my mother offers a perspective on when she gave birth to me and my siblings.

People of African descent have gone through a wide range of designations as to our ethnic name. We have been Colored. We have been Negro. During the 1960s and 1970s, we became Black. Being Black signaled a significant transition—a coming of age. Being Black was more than just an ethnic designation. It was an ideology and identification. Overlapping somewhat with being called Black, was the fairly "radical" choice of being called Afro-American (around the late 1960s). We have programs at universities that carry this name. And following a press conference called by Rev. Jesse Jackson in the late 1980s, many of us became African-Americans. There was a need or desire to be connected with a place, a continent or a country. Today, we are referred to as People of Color.

I personally have been referred to as all of the above before—Colored, Negro, Black, Afro-American, African-American and a Woman of Color. During my recent visit to Ghana, West Africa, I received a new designation. Who knows, in ten years there may be a new preference, but for our purpose, we'll use the designation, Woman of Color. I like this description. It is a succinct statement. It places both sex and ethnicity in a capsule form. Before this designation became vogue, I often referred to my people as colorful people—lively, ingenious, one-of-a-kind. Colorful.

We know what a woman of color looks like. What she looks like and what she does are parts of who she is. But what is she like? What is her heart, her passion, and her mission? Women of color are not a homogenous group. They do not all think the same, look the same or act the same. Among Black women is also tremendous diversity. Whether they are conservative, liberal or radical, they are deliberate and decisive and will do whatever is necessary to preserve what is most highly esteemed. A woman of color is passionate.

As a professor at a major research institution, many students call me for help with various assignments. Some of them share my research interest, which is, the Music of African-Americans, specifically, the African-American Sacred Music Tradition, and seek advice on their research projects. Others want to learn how to make effective presentations through the proper use of the voice, good posture and the appropriate use of gestures, etc. And others desperately need to find any professor who will allow them to conduct an interview for an impending assignment. I really enjoy teaching and working with the students and welcome any opportunity to impact their lives, whether it is for real scholarly pursuits or for a last-minute assignment.

The students approach me in a number of different ways. I have been interviewed as a member of the faculty; as a Black member of the faculty; as a female faculty member; and as a Black female faculty member. Now that I think about it, the university got a real bargain when I joined the faculty—at least four perspectives in one professor. What a deal!

The student interviewer typically selects me because of an activity that she associates me with, and is usually unaware of all of the other things I do. Their faces generally register some amazement when I share the many other things I am involved in. What I am to some, I am not to others.

In addition to being a wife (Mrs. Harold D. Davis) and mother to four children (Kirstie, Jonathan, Ashley and Charity, who all call me something different—Mother, Mama, Mom and Mommy), I perform a lot of other roles—many of which have unique titles associated with them. To many students, I am Professor Davis, Dr. Davis and/or Mrs. Davis. To some students, I am Mother, Doc, Mammadoc, and/or Ma'am. To my church family, I am Sister Davis. As a concert artist, I am Ms. Davis or Ollie Watts Davis. I answer by a lot of different titles depending upon who's calling.

During the more formal student interviews, where I am Professor Davis or Dr. Davis, there are usually a lot of questions regarding my personal life and work. They want to know where I'm from, how I came to Illinois and how I balance having a family, the professorate and an active performing career. They are curious to find out any pointers or secrets on how to do it all.

Besides questions concerning my personal life and work, they ask a set of questions about being female and being black. There is a great amount of intrigue surrounding these two elements. This is a hot topic right now that is enjoying a great deal of interest.

The questions about being a woman of color are usually similar. The students want to know what specific challenges I have faced that I attribute to my being black and a woman. I try to use these opportunities to set crooked records straight. My response always includes a historical, as well as a contemporary perspective. I remember the shoulders that I stand upon by citing the legacy that I am committed to. I remember my ancestors, those heroes and sheroes from the distant past and the not so distant past. I passionately herald how important it is that our generation carry the torch that lit our paths, and guarantee that the torch is passed on to future generations. I generally close my comments by issuing a challenge for the students to seize every opportunity before them, always give something back to the community, build into the life of someone else and never forget the shoulders upon which they stand.

In my more than ten years as a professor, there was one interview that I will never forget. A young Caucasian student, studying broadcast journalism, appeared at my studio one afternoon. Her mission was to conduct an interview for an assignment on Black female faculty members. After some preliminary dialogue, she got down to the business at hand. Her leading question to me was "How has being a woman of color served as a disadvantage for you?" She wanted to know "how being a woman of color had held me back in my personal and professional life." I remember taking some time before answering her. I needed to digest all of what she was saying. After gathering my thoughts, I remember beginning with something like this:

> *I have never considered being a woman of color to be a disadvantage. On the contrary, I regard my sex and my ethnicity among my greatest assets. I received both distinctions at birth. I view them as gifts that I gratefully receive. I have a unique perspective because of this that others need to learn from. My invitation to join the faculty of this University was not because they were seeking to hire a disadvantaged individual. Conversely, my appointment came because of what I could contribute to the intellectual life of this institution. You, as well as every other student I come in contact with are beneficiaries of my womanness and my blackness. Through my unique gifts, abilities and perspective, you are enlightened.*

The interview proceeded rather nicely, but I'll never forget her opening question. This was the first time anyone had ever suggested to me that being a woman of color was a disadvantage. I grew up in a home where I was regarded as a gift. Period! My mother loved her sons and she loved her daughters. I was not expendable because I was a Black female. I had never entertained the idea that my being a woman of color placed me at a disadvantage. It never occurred to me to have an inferiority mentality.

At the time I graduated from high school, I found myself in a unique position—I was considered a double minority, Black and a woman. I was told that there were many opportunities such as scholarships and nontraditional fields of study for me to pursue. I was encouraged to capitalize on everything. And I did. I never liked the term minority, but I intended to enjoy this coveted status for as long as it lasted. (Some people believe that because you are black and female, you have to be better than everyone else. This is emotionally exhausting and not at all possible. I believe that you should be your personal best. This is attainable).

I don't deny that there are challenges to being a woman of color. I am more often misunderstood than understood. People want to know "What does she want?" On a daily basis I contend with the various isms—racism, sexism, classism, etc. that plague my day and time. But I am not consumed by the ills of the world in which I live. I was born for such a time as this. I call an injustice out by telling it like it is. I offer an appropriate response and keep on pushing. I know my work. I do it well. I also know my rights and responsibilities. I don't make issues unless I need to. Then I make sure that others know that I know how to handle whatever situation I need to handle. I see myself as well-able to meet all opportunities and obstacles that come before me with strength and dignity.

I was created to be a woman of color, for such a time as this. I am here because the world needs a woman of color. There is a void that only I can fill. There are services that only I can perform. You are also exactly who you are because of a purpose that only you can fulfill. You have your own area of influence. You are created for your time. I receive being a woman of color as a gift. I wouldn't have it any other way.

I have known the women of many lands and nations. I have known, seen, and lived beside them, but none have I known more sweetly feminine, more unansweringly loyal, more desperately earnest, and more instinctively pure in body and in soul than the daughters of my African-American mothers. W.E.B. DUBOIS (1920)

Questions

1. What ethnic designation or name do you prefer to be called?

2. What kind of culture or ideology does this name represent?

3. How many different names do you answer to?

4. Do you celebrate your ancestors?

5. How do you view your ethnicity, as an advantage or disadvantage?

6. Do you have an inferior or superiority mentality in any area?

7. How well do you feel you understand or relate with people from different ethnic groups than your own?

8. Are you consumed by the ills of your world or are you an overcomer?

9. Do you feel that there is a void in this world that only you can fill?

10. Are you happy with yourself just as you are?

Mother Wit

One race has not accomplished anymore than any other race, for God could not be just and at the same time make one race inferior of the other. CARTER G. WOODSON

The true worth of a race must be measured by the character of its womanhood.
MARY MCLEOD BETHUNE

When you educate a man you educate an individual, but when you educate a woman, you educate a nation.
JOHNETTA B. COLE

In every race, in every nation, and in every clime, in every period of history, there is always an eager-eyed group of youthful patriots who seriously set themselves to right the wrongs done to their race or nation or sect or sometimes to art or self-expression. No race or nation can advance without them. ALICE DUNBAR-NELSON

We weren't pushing Black is beautiful. We just showed it.
KATHERINE DUNHAM

I did not know whether to be proud of my color or ashamed of it. . .I was a changeling, presenting different faces to different people, and to this day, I am two or three people.
LENA HORNE

Music was, and perhaps still is, the area of my life where the questions of color comes second and the question of whether you play good or not is the one you have to answer as a test of admission into society. LENA HORNE

228

28
Standard English:
Spoken by Those Who Do Business
(the language of money)

$$\approx$$

Before our children were born, my husband and I decided that we would not talk "baby talk" to them. We would raise the pitch of our voices and talk softly at times and excitedly at other times, but we would leave out the goo-goo, ga-ga. We knew that they would pick up our dialect anyway and didn't feel that adding unintelligible chatter to their vocabulary was really necessary. I remember one time when my youngest daughter, Charity, asked her father, "What you fittin' to do Dad?" Astonished, he looked at her and then asked me, "Where did she get that from? Where did she hear that?" I told him that she had picked it up from him, that he said it all the time. He denied it of course, but had to repent later when the other children chimed in, "Yes you do Dad." He had heard it from his father, and now here was his daughter hearing it from her father.

Language links us. It connects us. Speaking a person's language is one of the most effective ways of breaking down barriers and showing that there is a degree of understanding between the two of you. I have studied a number of foreign languages, and whenever I meet someone from one of those countries, I try to speak to her in her native tongue. Even if I completely blow the accent and nuance, the effort to try to communicate on their terms is appreciated. It's a nice gesture that doesn't cost me anything but a little vulnerability.

Whether you've studied a foreign language or not, you may be multilingual too. You may speak two dialects, and perhaps even more. You speak the English language that has been filtered through a number of different experiences: that of your family, your friends, your workplace and school. You are probably proficient in writing in these various dialects as well. Words that are spelled the same or that sound the same may have different meanings depending upon the context. It is very important that you have a good sense of place, and know when to use which dialect. You should know how to speak effectively in a variety of contexts. Do not throw away what you grew up with. There's a place for it. Enhance it. But always remember that what's appropriate in the 'hood is not necessarily appropriate in the classroom. You must be adaptable.

It is always acceptable to respond in standard English, even if you reason mentally in your dialect. We may come to an understanding through our comfort language (dialect), but when we express that understanding to the larger audience at school or at work, we need to be able to be articulate in the accepted language—standard English. I teach a number of students whose native language is not English. I am amazed at how quickly they acquire a proficiency in the English language. They achieve a greater command of English than many native speakers in both writing and speaking. But even though they acquire good facility in English, they keep their native languages as their point of reference. Whenever I give them a direction or instruction, I can see and almost hear them mentally going through a translation process. They take my English statements, translate them into their native language, gain an understanding

230

in their native language, translate their understanding into English, then respond to me in English. They are able to do this so successfully because they know their language and understand the English language.

Language is power and those who have a good command of language are powerful. While the purpose of language is to help us communicate, we also have to consider what is appropriate. It is inappropriate to use street language, with slang vocabulary and altered meanings at a job interview, at a professional meeting or in the classroom. Unless you have the luxury of having an interpreter at your disposal, you had best learn how to be articulate in standard English, otherwise referred to as the King's English. I doubt that you can afford your personal interpreter at this point, so I suggest you find a book of English grammar and start studying.

Learn to speak and write well. Build your vocabulary in these ways:

1. Reading. Go to your school library and get a list of suggested reading materials for your grade level. Read at least 20 minutes a day.

2. Listen to books on tape. Go to the public library and get a novel by a famous author on tape. Instead of doing your chores to music, listen to a book.

3. Listen to the radio. Listen to interviews, and documentaries on the public radio stations.

4. Watch documentaries on your public TV station.

5. Buy a student dictionary. Start with A and read. Whenever you run across a word you don't know, write it down with its definition. Use it in a sentence or conversation.

I learned the construction of the English language by diagramming sentences. You're probably wondering, *"What?"* I don't know why this method was discarded, but I believe it needs to be brought back. Diagramming a sentence enabled you to see the sentence as a diagram with the various parts of speech linked in a certain way. You can literally see how it all relates—how subjects and verbs agree; what adverbs and adjectives modify; where to place definite and indefinite articles, prepositional phrases, and so forth. What you see visually reinforces what you learn mentally.

Your generation has traded in these fundamentals of good writing and speaking skills for the freedom to think and write creatively. Creativity has never been a problem, but how to effectively put the creativity down on paper or intelligibly deliver it in a speech remains a mystery. If you have difficulty in English, composition or language arts classes, go to your teacher and ask him or her if they will show you how to diagram a sentence. It can't hurt, and it might just help you.

Standard English is the language spoken by those who do serious business in America. It is the language of the dollar. Do not concern yourself with those who will ridicule you for "talking proper." Speak properly all the way to the bank. A good fundamental vocabulary and functional construction skills are crucial to your financial future. You must take the necessary time and learn the fundamentals of the language, which include: spelling rules, parts of speech, sentence structure, punctuation rules, capitalization rules and the features of writing and speaking. You can find an English grammar book in any bookstore or library. Check it out.

Questions

1. What vocabulary have you picked up from your orientation family?

2. Are there any words you say that you don't want to say?

3. When was the last time you learned a new word?

4. Do you own and use a dictionary?

5. How many books do you read in a year?

6. Do you try to talk to others in their language?

7. Do you use the same language in every setting?

8. Can you talk to a professional person without feeling intimidated?

9. Are you able to write out your creative thoughts?

10. What will you do to increase your language skills?

Mother Wit

Few high school students look upon the language which they speak and write as an art. Yet it is, or ought to be, the noblest of all the arts, looked upon with respect, even with reverence, and used always with care, courtesy, and the deepest respect.
MARY ELLEN CHASE

Education is a precondition to survival in America today.
MARIAN WRIGHT EDLEMAN

Let your conversation be gracious as well as sensible, for then you will have the right answer for everyone. PAUL OF TARSUS

Everyone hears only what he understands. GOETHE

Words embolden. Words help us with future conquests. Words enlarge our spirit. CARL ROWAN

The limits of my language are the limits of my mind. All I know is what I have words for.
LUDWIG WITTGENSTEIN

In this country, business is conducted in White English. That is a fact of life. You don't "get down" when talking with the chairman of the board; you don't greet him with a big "Hey!" and a brothers' handshake. You don't punctuate every sentence that makes sense with a "right on." BILL COSBY

By inflection you can say much more than your words do.
MALCOLM S. FORBES

Part VI

Addressing What Lies Ahead

Tell your children they're not going to jive their way up the career ladder. They have to work their way up hard. There's no fast elevator to the top.
Marian Wright Edelman

29
Your Work Ethic
(needed: more than a pretty hand)

H ave you ever heard the phrase *"if you want something done right, you better do it yourself?"* It is an old-school saying and it is not a compliment. This phrase is usually made as a judgment or indictment against someone's work. It suggests that there is some dissatisfaction with the quality of a job. Whoever makes the statement feels that they should have done the work themselves, or that they could have done a better job. This phrase is not something you want said about your work.

People can be very unforgiving about poor quality work. If your work doesn't measure up because you do not have the know-how, that's understandable. But if your work doesn't measure up because you do not have the want-to, that is inexcusable. Lack of ability is one thing, lack of desire is something else.

Lack of desire is often revealed as a lackadaisical attitude that says *"I'm doing you a favor"* or *"I don't want to be here anyway."* This attitude is commonly found among those in service-oriented positions, such as cashiers, retailers and waitresses. All of these are positions where personal work ethic can make or break a business. You cannot afford to have a lackadaisical attitude. It's much too expensive. It will cost you many opportunities.

Take a look at the following scenario and see if you can identify any lackadaisical characteristics.

A young lady decides she wants a job. She fills out applications all over town—at the mall, grocery stores and fast-food restaurants. She finally gets a call from Buddy's Burger Bar. She goes in for the interview and is hired. She is scheduled to start the next day.

Week One
The first few days are great—she gets there on time, with a big smile on her face, ready to flip burgers and drop fries. Payday is coming and she is all excited. She gets her first check and is disappointed because it is 25% less than she was expecting. In her calculations, she failed to deduct taxes and social security from her gross.

Week Two
She is running late. She calls ahead and lets them know that she's on her way. She gets to work and is pleasant, but not as perky as before. Flipping burgers and dropping fries is not as exciting now as it was when she thought her take-home pay would be more.

Week Three
She's running late again, but doesn't bother to call ahead. When she finally gets there, she is unapologetic about being late. She walks in with a funky attitude that says "don't say nothing to me." She goes about the day doing her job half-heartedly and acting like she doesn't want to be there. After a while, she asks if she can leave early because she has something to do. After two weeks of this type of performance, she is relieved (fired) of her duties. She doesn't understand why

she was fired. She says "they are wrong, and should be glad to have me there working for pocket change."

There is a lot going on in this scenario—two things that I want to point out.

1. This young lady hired herself and she fired herself. She was diligent and tenacious about finding a job—putting in applications all over town. Keeping the job and advancing required the same tenacity and diligence. She determined that she was being treated unfairly and let her disappointment affect her performance. She didn't know the future. Perhaps her supervisor would have promoted her had she earned it.

2. She attached a pricetag to her work. She worked hard when she thought she would make a lot of money. But when she found out that her pay wasn't exactly what she thought it would be, she adjusted her work ethic. She devalued herself and her work. In other words she thought, if this is all I'm going to be paid, this is all that I'm going to do. Everyone has this temptation, but it is very important not to yield to it. I will never be adequately paid for my work. I accept what is given but it doesn't pay me for the heart, soul, passion and love that I put into my work. My work ethic is priceless. There is no amount great enough to adequately compensate me. There is no amount too insufficient. I do what I do whether given much or little. It will not affect the quality of my work.

A good work ethic is a desire to put forth your best effort consistently, regardless of who is watching or whether you'll receive any recognition for it. It is an attitude—your mental commitment to excellence, that is revealed through your outward demonstration. It is what you do, not what you promise or talk about doing. It is where your walk meets your talk, where the rubber hits the road. Your work ethic is your personal standard of performance.

I learned the importance of work and the work ethic early. Part of my inspiration for acquiring skills and developing a work ethic was the fact that I had been prophesied over, as had my brothers and sisters. What my mother said, came to pass. She prophesied that at age 18, our plates would be broken. This was not a literal breaking of plates, but it was the metaphor she used to let us know that we were expected to be able to provide for ourselves by that time. Two options were available to us—we could either go to college or go to work. To stay at home ("lay up at home," as she called it) and not be productive was not even a consideration. She reasoned that if you could be drafted into the military at 18 and trusted to defend the country, you ought to be able to do something productive and support yourself—in other words, fend for yourself. I, along with my siblings, fulfilled this prophecy. One by one, we left home after high school graduation, and went either to college or to work.

The threat of homelessness and hunger was not credible. We knew that we were loved and whatever we needed, would be provided somehow. But we also knew that we weren't entitled. This prophecy was Mama's spin on teaching us an important principle.

Principle: Nobody owes you anything! You are not entitled to anything that you do not work for.

We were able to fulfill this prophecy because we had been prepared. We were raised with expectations and encouraged along the way to prepare for our future. If you thought that when you reached age 18 your meals were going to be cut off, it would be wise of you to make sure you learned how to do some things and do them well along the way. I acquired some practical skills. I learned how to sew, cook, clean, type and take short-hand. I had no intentions of becoming a domestic (housecleaner and cook), seamstress or secretary, but I made good use of my time. This leads to another helpful principle for developing a good work ethic.

Principle: Make good use of your time. Acquire life-skills. Trade your time for teaching. Be a volunteer. Apprentice yourself. Work for free to acquire a skill and experience.

For 18 years, my siblings and I saw a good work ethic modeled. We saw standards upheld. Whatever our grandmother and mother put their hands to do, they did with their might and to the best of their ability. They took pride in their work. We learned that there is a great deal of esteem to be derived from hard work. We were taught that there was only one way to do something—the right way. To say that you had tried, didn't mean anything. You were to stay at a task until it was done correctly. To say that you had worked for a long time didn't matter either. You were not finished until it passed their inspection. A job well done was expected. We could not let just anything go.

Your work is an extension of you. Always put forth your best effort. If there is something that you do not understand about a task or assignment, ask for an explanation, get clear directions and then get to work. You are responsible for the finished product. Don't settle for just presenting anything and sell yourself cheaply. People form opinions about you based on the work you present. Your work should represent you well without requiring any explanations.

My work ethic has served me greatly throughout my life. There were some specific principles that I learned that helped me to develop a healthy concept of work. I encourage you to consider them as guidelines as you develop your concept of the work ethic.

1. Nobody owes you anything! You are not entitled to anything that you do not work for.

2. Make good use of your time. Apprentice yourself. Volunteer and work for free to acquire life-skills and experience.

3. Be diligent and work hard wherever you are now. If you are a student, be the best student that you can be. Student life is your first job. Make sure that your work is commendable.

4. Honor your commitments. Be dependable, reliable and trustworthy. Establish a good track record.

5. Be responsible. Be punctual. And be professional. Remember that your work is a reflection of you.

Questions

1. How would you describe your work ethic?

2. Are you satisfied with your work ethic?

3. Has a lackadaisical attitude ever cost you anything?

4. Would you rather have someone give you something or work for it yourself?

5. Did anyone ever threaten to "break your plate"?

6. Have you been raised with expectations and encouraged along the way to prepare for your future?

7. How do you feel about the principles given in the chapter?

8. Name five women you know who display a good work ethic.

9. Are you currently making good use of your time?

Mother Wit

Tell our children they're not going to jive their way up the career ladder. They have to work their way up hard. There's no fast elevator to the top. MARIAN WRIGHT EDELMAN

Rest and play are the desserts of life. Work is the meal. It is only a child who dreams of a diet of dessert alone. HAROLD MAYFIELD

Lazy men are soon poor; hard workers get rich. A wise youth makes hay while the sun shines, but what a shame to see a lad who sleeps away his hour of opportunity. KING SOLOMON

Hard work means prosperity; only a fool idles away his time. KING SOLOMON

For even when we were with you, this we commanded you, that if any would not work, neither should he eat. PAUL OF TARSUS

The only place where success comes before work is a dictionary. VIDAL SASSOON

Show me a man who cannot bother to do little things and I'll show you a man who cannot be trusted to do big things. LAWRENCE D. BELL

Good is not good where better is expected. THOMAS FULLER

He that can work is born a king of something. THOMAS CARLYLE

244

30
My First Job
(a personal story)

I was sixteen years old, it was summertime and I was bored stiff. After hanging around the house for a week or so, doing nothing really productive, I finally convinced my mother to let me get a job for the summer. There weren't many choices to begin with, and by the time I got permission, the county had filled all of the office positions. The only jobs left were crew jobs, where you pick up litter along the highway. As desperate as it sounds, I applied for a crew job. I wanted to work and anything was better than nothing.

On the day that I was supposed to go and actually fill out the application, I was told to wear old clothes—they suggested blue jeans, tennis shoes, long socks, long-sleeved shirts and a scarf or hat—because I might start working that same day. I dressed in my work gear and was ready to go to the office when my mother looked at me and asked a question like only she can ask a question. *"Where do you think you're going?"* Her question was loaded. It wasn't really a question at all. She was telling me that I wasn't going anywhere looking like that. I told her the information I had received concerning the type of work I would be doing, which explained why I was dressed the way I was. As

if she didn't hear a word I had said, she asked, "Are *you* going to apply for a job?" I answered, "Yes." Then she added, "Then, *dress* for the job you are applying for." I knew what she meant, so I went to my room and dressed for the job I wanted to apply for, which was an office job. By insisting that I dress appropriately, my mother was teaching me valuable lessons. I learned that even when you are applying for a job, you must look like you can do the job, like you belong in the position you are applying for and that you deserve an opportunity to demonstrate your ability. I
learned not to doubt the influence your presence might have on a situation.

Well, I dressed for the office position in a light blue skirt, white blouse, hose and dress shoes. I didn't know exactly what my mother had up her sleeve, but I knew I wouldn't be starting crew work that day. On the way to the employment office, I felt a bit ridiculous. I had talked to the lady on the phone. I heard and understood what she had said. There were no more office jobs. But, I did as my mother said anyway, even though I thought I knew better.

There were many teenagers in the office when we arrived. I knew some of them. They looked at me wondering why I was there in a skirt and stockings. I was wondering the same thing too. I tried to avoid eye contact after a while and just sat there with my mother, waiting my turn.

I heard the secretary give several young people the same speech regarding the crew positions—when they would be picked up, what to wear, where the different work sites were and when they would start. Finally, my turn came. I walked up to the counter, stated my name and expected the same routine. To my surprise, the script was altered.

Without looking up from her papers, the secretary asked me, "So you are here for a job?" To which I replied, "Yes Ma'am." She then looked up at me, saw how I was dressed and said,

"You do realize that the only jobs we have left are crew jobs along the highway?" I answered, "Yes, Ma'am." There was a pause, and she just looked at me. She then asked me if I could type. I told her I could and she told me to have a seat for a minute. She called the Social Security office and said, "We have a young lady here who can type. Can you please find something for her to do in your office this summer—typing, filing, answering the telephone, anything?" After a few minutes, she called me back to the counter and told me that I would be working at the Social Security office as an office assistant and would start the next day. My professional dress and demeanor had earned me a summer job in a nice air-conditioned office where I could use my skills instead of baking in the sun while picking up trash along the highway. I had my mother to thank once again.

I looked back at my mother from the counter, and she said nothing, but her expression was screaming, "What did I tell you?"

I learned many lessons that day. Three that I want to share with you.

1. Always have a good attitude. While I was not overly excited about the possibility of working along the highway, I never let the lady interviewing me know that. I showed a good attitude the entire time. Are you keeping your attitude in check?

2. Wear good attire. The clothes I wore weren't new nor were they name brand. They were clean, neat and appropriate for the job. The dress that I wore told the interviewer a whole lot about me. What are you saying about yourself based upon how you are dressing?

3. Have good abilities. Learning to type in the 7th and 8th grades certainly paid off in this situation. Things that you are learning may not seem relevant now, but you'll need them later. Learn all that you can now. Develop yourself. Your gifts and abilities will open up many opportunities for you.

Questions

1. If you are a student, do you realize that your current business is your school work?

2. Are you dependable?

3. What is your attitude about dressing professionally for work?

4. What kind of job do you want to have?

5. What are the benefits of dressing for the job that you want to have?

6. What are the benefits of being on time?

7. What do you learn about human nature from the author's interaction with the woman at the desk?

8. How does your vocabulary and appearance serve you?

9. Reflect on the three lessons that the author shares.

Mother Wit

You have only one chance to make a first impression. Make it count. MARKITA ANDREWS

We make a living by what we get, but we make a life by what we give. BARBARA HARRIS

Do the best you can in every task, no matter how unimportant it may seem at the time. No one learns more about a problem than the person at the bottom. SANDRA DAY O'CONNOR

Luck is being ready for the chance. J. FRANK DOBIE

Putting confidence in an unreliable man is like chewing with a sore tooth, or trying to run on a broken foot. KING SOLOMON

Today's global marketplace demands highly skilled, effective managers. EARL G. GRAVES

I above all believe in work—systematic and tireless.
W. E. B. DUBOIS

Thinking is the hardest work there is, which is probably the the reason so few engage in it. HENRY FORD

Look at a day when you are supremely satisfied at the end. It's not a day when you lounge around doing nothing. It's when you've had everything to do, and you've done it.
MARGARET THATCHER

The many of us who attain what we may and forget those who help us along the line — we've got to remember that there are so many others to pull along the way. The further they go, the further we all go.

Jackie Robinson

31
Lifting as You Climb
(empowering others)

I am not a self-made woman. I do not profess to have *picked myself up by my bootstraps*. Many people helped me when I couldn't help myself. I stand on the shoulders of many, with my mother, Ramona Sereta Crider Ross (1931-1979), and my mentor, Ethel Jean Caffie-Austin providing the principal foundation. I am eternally grateful for their instruction and influence. They gave me what they had.

I am a rich sister, not because I possess an abundance of things, but because of what possesses me. I am entrusted with a legacy that values truth, faith, a strong work ethic and an obligation to serve. I have benefited from those strategically placed in my life who were willing to help me in various ways. The best way for me to remember what has been done for me is to do what I can for someone else. I am committed to lifting others as I climb. I am my sister's keeper.

I was impressed with a sense of duty at an early age. When I was eight years old, my oldest sister, Linda, graduated from high school and moved to Washington, D.C. She left home, but her heart was never far from us. After she got settled, she sent for me and my siblings to come and visit. I remember going to the National Theater with her to see my first Broadway musical, *"Bubblin' Brown Sugar,"* and my first theatrical performance, the one-man show, *Paul Robeson*, portrayed by James Earl Jones. We all benefited from her generous love and commitment to family. This tradition of reaching back was continued when my sister Anita left for the university. I have fond memories of spending time with her on campus. She introduced me to bowling at the student center, the Mountain Lair, and is responsible for my ears being pierced. My success is made possible by those who have preceded me—some people I know well, others I've read bout and still others I don't know at all. There were those who did not enjoy privilege nor opportunity, but prayed that we might. And because of their prayers, their struggle and their endurance, doors were opened for us. No history book nor televison documentary could have impressed me more with this truth than what I experienced on my first trip to the real South.

I was at Auburn University in Auburn, Alabama to present a concert. I attended a church service the morning prior to my performance and was introduced to two members from the only three Black families who lived in the entire city of Auburn. I felt their pride in my accomplishment as we greeted one another and they gave their best wishes for my concert the following day. During the recital, I looked for them in the audience. They were there. Proud. Smiling. With chests puffed out. You would have thought that I was a close relative by their enthusiam and embrace. Their words, "We're so proud of you," brought tears to my eyes following the performance. My success had brought them pride and distinction and they were able to share in the moment. I again realized the connectedness of people and was reminded of my responsibility to my people.

I grew up in a town at a time when, if one did well, everyone rejoiced. Good news about a homeboy or homegirl spread quickly from house to house. One may receive the recognition and carry the trophy, but all share in the victory. Achievement was a community affair. It felt good to be included among *Mount Hope's finest*—a sort of community "Who's Who." My return home to give the Commencement address at my high school is among my proudest moments. It is a real honor to be esteemed in your home town.

With honor comes a sense of duty and responsibility. I shared earlier that my mother encouraged me to go as far as I could and be all that I could be. And with that she added, "Don't forget where you came from or those who follow after you." I learned early that whatever success I achieved was to be enjoyed by all. Those who express interest in my field of endeavor can expect me to offer helpful suggestions and advice. I have a moral obligation to lift others as I climb. There is no threat to me when I help someone else. No one can take that which has been purposed for me. I am so glad that I was taught this truth—if I win, it doesn't mean someone else has to lose. Or in order for someone else to win, it doesn't mean that I must lose. There can be a win-win situation.

I inherited a rich legacy upon which to build and to uphold. I've had great teachers—my parents, family and friends. It wasn't enough for us to do as well as them, we were encouraged to go beyond them. We were expected to gain wisdom from our elders and add it to the opportunities we had. Their shoulders provided us with a jumping off point.

I have been fortunate to have many people contribute to my life. Some things I have learned directly, and some indirectly. I know how wonderful it feels to have someone who really wants to help you and who is willing to share everything they know with you. I have also experienced someone withholding vital information because of a fear that you might surpass them. I have modeled my philosophy after those who deliberately sought to teach me, to empower me.

When I was a junior in college, I entered a twentieth century music contest. The music was very difficult. It was my first experience with repertoire (music) that I felt like I was seeing for the first time, weeks after I had been practicing it. The piano accompaniment was as demanding, if not more demanding, as the vocal line. I was fortunate to have a piano professor from a neighboring college agree to rehearse with me. Once a week, I took a forty mile bus ride to her campus to rehearse. As we neared the end of our sessions, I asked her—"Dr. Giles, what do I owe you?" I will never forget her response. She said, "Oh, just go and be successful. When you're successful, then you can buy me an ice cream cone."

I adopted this philosophy as my own. The best way to show gratitude is to take what you've been taught and be successful.

Now it is your turn. It is your turn to do for others what has been done for you. You owe it to those who have preceded you and those who follow you, to be the best that you can be and share all that you have received with those who need it. It is our obligation to share with those who are alongside us and who follow after.

Whatever you achieve or accomplish should benefit more than yourself. Can you be trusted to continue the flow of blessing? All who follow after you should be blessed because of you. I am blessed because I can be trusted to be a blessing. Can you be trusted?

As you climb, I want you to remember two things:

1. Always remember that someone ahead of you has paved the way for you, and
2. Don't let grass grow on the path that you make. Keep someone on the path.

Questions

1. Do you feel that you are a self-made person? Why or why not?

2. Upon whose shoulders do you stand?

3. What woman or women are you eternally grateful to for their influence in your life?

4. Have you been entrusted with a legacy?

5. In what ways have you witnessed the "connectedness" of people?

6. Are you gaining wisdom from your elders and adding it to the opportunities that come your way?

7. Are you committed to lifting others as you climb?

Mother Wit

I suppose I might insist on making issues of things. But that is not my nature, and I always bear in mind that my mission is to leave behind me the kind of impression that will make it easier for those who follow. MARIAN ANDERSON

A good heart is better than all the heads in the world. EDWARD BULWER-LYTTON

Only a life lived for others is a life worthwhile. ALBERT EINSTEIN

A hand up is better than a hand out. SYBIL MOBLEY

Success is not defined by the number of servants you have, but by how many people you serve. RALPH D. ABERNATHY

Much is required from those to whom much is given, for their responsibility is greater. JESUS CHRIST

Success always leaves footprints. BOOKER T. WASHINGTON

I've benefitted from many scholarships. A number of people paid a lot of dues for me to do what I do. I feel it's my responsibility to give back. WYNTON MARSALIS

No matter what accomplishments you make, somebody helps you. ALETHA GIBSON

The only justification for ever looking down on somebody is to pick them up. JESSE JACKSON

32
A Mother Should Teach Her Daughter How to Die Easily
(making ready)

It was a cold, snowy, December day. Visibility wasn't great, temperatures were dropping and the meteorologists (weather people) were encouraging everyone to stay in. I picked my youngest daughter up from school and we headed for home. Our car was sliding all over the road. We ran into the curb several times trying to stop and keep from sliding into an intersection. At first it didn't bother her too much. She was accustomed to some sliding fun when she rode with her Dad. But, at one point, the car did a 180 degree turn. This was a bit much for her to take. She sat up and with a tearful voice said, *"Mommy, I don't want to die."* I knew that this was the right time for me to make sure she knew how to die.

The way you learn how to die is by learning how to live. The best teacher is a good example. A mother who models a life of integrity, love and commitment to her family plants precious seeds in the lives of her daughters.

Integrity is a rich heritage. You may not inherit money or

material things, but a rich heritage is a true treasure. There should be no secret where you stand on issues of right and wrong. Your integrity should be common knowledge to those who live, work or hang out with you.

You can inherit a good name and heritage but you must individually and personally build on what you have been given. Many children who come from good homes are careless with how they protect the family name and reputation. Other children come from backgrounds where the name carried very little weight and there were character issues related to the family in the past. Regardless of what you start out with, you can build a wonderful reputation that will have people speak well of you. What I am saying is, don't make the preacher lie at your funeral. Live a life that presents those who remain with a dilemma. On one hand they miss you and are sad, and on the other hand, the thought of you brings happy memories.

There is an eerie feeling and degree of discomfort when the subject of death and dying comes up. It is an unavoidable fact of life. Each day, all around the world, people of all ages, cultures, genders and economic statuses die. Because death is inevitable, we should all make ready. Make sure that you have an insurance policy that will cover the expenses of your funeral. Most children are covered on their parent's insurance policies, but as soon as you are an adult, get your own coverage so that there will not be a financial burden on your family and friends. A decent funeral costs about $5,000.00.

Every mother should teach her daughter the necessary facts about death and dying. This is important and will impact the type of life that a daughter chooses to live. I have never seen anyone take her last breath. I have no curiosities about that. I believe that death is between a woman and her maker. It is not necessary for me to be a witness. But I am told by some who have been witnesses at deathbeds that there is a marked difference between the death of the righteous and the death of a fool. As the person lived so the person died. If a woman had lived like a mad woman, she died like a mad woman, fitful, fighting and afraid. If a woman had lived a peaceful life, she died in a peaceful manner.

The only understanding that my little girl had about death was that it was painful and difficult. To her, death occurred as a result of being in a bad situation. To use her own words, she said *"it doesn't look like any fun to be in."* Television, movies, magazines, newspapers and even cartoons portray dying in graphic, violent and painful ways. And it does happen for some just like that. We live in a world where the value of life has diminished for some to such a degree that there is little regard for one's own life and no regard for another's life.

I calmed Charity's fears by assuring her of the faith that is dear to our family and for the remainder of our trip home we talked about our faith (belief system). Do you have a belief system regarding death? Do you understand it? Have you discussed it with your parents or religious leaders? Take the time to settle the issue now while you are very much among the living.

Questions

1. Have you ever had a close call with death?

2. What emotions come to mind when you think about dying? How prepared are you for death?

3. If you were to die today, what would be the most significant contribution that you would leave behind?

4. How do you want to be remembered by future generations?

5. Do you feel that the author picked the right time to talk to her daughter about the delicate issue of death?

6. Do you believe that a person dies like they live?

7. Whose death has been most significant to you? How did that death change you?

8. Do you feel that life is valued in our society?

9. How do you plan to live a full life?

Mother Wit

A mother is not someone to lean on but a person to make leaning unnecessary. DOROTHY CANFIELD FISHER

You don't get to choose how you're going to die or when. You can only decide how you are going to live. Now. JOAN BAEZ

The bitterest tears shed over graves are for words left unsaid and deeds left undone. HARRIET BEECHER STOWE

I'm ready to close this chapter of my life. BILLIE HOLIDAY

At its most basic root, the death or disintegration of one's parents is a harsh reminder of one's own mortality.
JANET HARRIS

My interest is in the future because I am going to spend the rest of my life there. CHARLES F. KETTERING

Teach us to number our days that we may apply our hearts to wisdom. KING SOLOMON

It is better to spend your time at funerals than at festivals. For you are going to die and it is a good thing to think about it while there is still time. KING SOLOMON

Do not take life too seriously. You will never get out of it alive.
ELBERT HUBBARD

A man's dying is more the survivors' affair than his own.
WOODY ALLEN

*You must do the thing you
think you cannot do.*

Eleanor Roosevelt

33
The Closing Chapter
(the afterword)

of making many books there is no end. KING SOLOMON

If you are reading this page, I want to be the first to congratulate you for hanging in there. There may have been times when you didn't feel that you could relate to what was written, and that's okay. You finished the course. Trust me, you will understand it better by and by.

As I bring this book to a close, it is with some reluctance. I feel like I do when my children go away on a trip. I wonder if they have what they need, if they remembered all that they were supposed to—knowing full well that something will be left behind. With this writing, I wonder if our talks were what you needed. Have we covered enough of the important stuff? I trust that we did. I realize that we can't cover it all.

You be the judge. If there is an area where you need specific answers and significant help, compose a chapter on it. Your assignment now is to review and respond to what has been written and then compile a list of chapter titles that also need to be addressed. Be a scholar and conduct your own research.

Gather insight and wisdom from primary sources (women older than you) and secondary sources (books, articles, etc.). Glean principles and perspectives from your pursuit. Wrap up your findings with your personal summary and opinion, and share all that you learn with someone else.

I realize that I have not addressed every issue that you are confronted with or will confront. There would be no end to my writing if I attempted to do that. I have elected to share specific lessons from my life with the hope that you will benefit from my transparency. This book is my story—my attempt to fully understand it. Now it is time for you to write yours.

Questions

1. Did this book cover enough of the important stuff?

2. Which chapters were most helpful to you?

3. Did you benefit form the author's transparency?

4. Why do you believe the author asks you to share what you learn with someone else?

5. Completing this book is proof that you have skills and are interested in getting ahead in life. What book or self-improvement related task will you take on next?

6. Are you ready to write your story?

Please consider sending a copy of your story or a letter to the author. Send it to the publisher's address found in the front of the book.

Mother Wit

Nothing in the world can take the place of persistence. Talent will not; nothing is more common than unsuccessful men of talent. Genius will not; unrewarded genius is almost a proverb. Education will not; the world is full of educated derelicts. Persistence and determination alone are omnipotent.
CALVIN COOLIDGE

I believe that the sign of maturity is accepting deferred gratification. PEGGY CAHN

You cannot teach a man anything; you can only help him find it within himself. GALILEO

You must do the thing you think you cannot do.
ELEANOR ROOSEVELT

People seldom improve when they have no other model but themselves to copy after. OLIVER GOLDSMITH

Our aim should be service, not success. BARBARA SMITH

It's not what you take but what you leave behind that defines greatness. EDWARD GARDNER

Notes:

Notes:

Notes:

Notes:_____

_____

_____

_____

_____

_____

_____

_____

_____

_____

_____

_____

_____

_____

_____

_____

_____

Notes:

Notes:_____
_____
_____
_____
_____
_____
_____
_____
_____
_____
_____
_____
_____
_____
_____
_____
_____
_____